Twelve Step R
Cognitive Behavioral Therapy

Understanding the Similarity of

Processes in

Twelve-Step Recovery

&

Cognitive Behavioral Therapy

Highest Regards

John E.

Get into Recovery

1st Edition

Twelve-Step Recovery and Cognitive Behavioral
Therapy
ISBN-13:978-1721623693
ISBN-10:1721623698
Jun 2018 Edition.

We are not affiliated with Alcoholics Anonymous or
any other 12 Step program.

'Admitted to God, to ourselves and to another human being the exact nature of our wrongs.'

'Were entirely ready to have God remove all these defects of character.'

Chapter Seven 133

Step Seven 133

'Humbly asked Him to remove our shortcomings.'

Chapter Eight 145

Step Eight 145

'Made a list of persons we had harmed, and became willing to make amends to them all.'

knowledge of His will for us and the power to carry that out.'

Chapter Twelve 192

Step Twelve..192

'Having had a spiritual awakening as the result of these steps, we tried to carry this message to alcoholics and to practice these principles in all our affairs'

Chapter Thirteen..203

CBT and Twelve-Step techniques.............................203

Further similarities and concepts 203

Prelude

Biological, psychological, social

Arguments

Do you believe in the Twelve Steps? Is addiction a disease? Is there a biological reason? Are people self-medicating? Are they mentally ill? Or is it their own fault and they deserve what they get? It's a harsh world with multiple opinions and maybe all of them have an element of truth. Research any addiction-treatment model and you will find fault and success stories with all of them. It breaks my heart that people are dying from addiction and many as a result of the medicines that are meant to be helping them. Treatment services that only believe in the model they deliver are contributing to the failure of our welfare systems. From the nurse who belittles someone for attending a self-help fellowship to the addict who is not welcome in a meeting because he/she may be on medication for depression. All of these and similar attitudes are killing people.

I could write that we are all guilty of this lack of joined-up working but this will only get a backlash from people who will argue that they could not possibly be contributing to the failure of treatment. 'It's everyone else,' they will cry. So, what's this book about and why am I writing it?

My main reason is to challenge people that there are similarities in what we all do as regards helping alcoholics or addicts. The focus of this book is on the Twelve Steps and CBT and you may argue that there is no connection but, I believe, that no one can argue that addiction has at least three main components.

1. **It is biological.** That is to say, part of the illness stems from the biological functioning of a person's body. There is brain chemistry involved, changes in brain structure, and genetic differences that influence human behavior. Which came first, the chicken or the egg? For some, the biological reasons will be as a result of their addiction and for others, it will be the cause.

2. **It is psychological.** That is to say, part of the illness stems from psychological causes. There are elements involved like emotional issues, lack of self-control, negative thinking, narcissism (self-centredness), and anxiety (fear). Again, what came first, the chicken or the egg? For some the psychological reasons will be a result of their addiction, for others, they will be the cause.

3. **It is social.** That is to say, part of the illness stems from social factors. There are elements involved such as culture, peer pressure, religion, social status, housing, economic status, technology, and access to treatment. Again, which came first? For some, the social reasons will be as a result of their addiction, for others they will be the cause.

If you wish to argue that it is only one of the above elements then fine, but maybe reading this book is not for you. I will also be touching on the spiritual aspects of recovery, and maybe that is a step too far. If you agree that the above aspects present themselves in the addict with varying degrees of impact, being different for each and every one of us, then you have to agree that a solution needs to cover all of those elements to be able to work.

Explanations and descriptions

For each of the Twelve Steps, I will be writing on aspects of the biopsychosocial model and how I see it relate to them. I am trying to explain all the connections that I see, and how I see them. I'm hopeful of educating at least some people who refuse to see the connections, or who bandy about the phrase 'evidence-based' when they wouldn't know a double-blind study from phenomenological research.

I shall start by covering the American Society of Addiction Medicine's (ASAM) definition of addiction. Many have written that this definition puts addiction into the medical-model category, 'It's about brains, not drugs,' says Dr Michael Miller, past president of ASAM, and it may be, but the long version of the description certainly covers all the different areas of a complex model.

'Addiction is a **primary**, **chronic** and **progressive** disease of **brain reward, motivation, memory** and **related circuitry**. Dysfunction in these circuits leads to characteristic **biological, psychological, social** and **spiritual manifestations**'.

'This is reflected in an individual pathologically pursuing reward and/or relief by substance use and other behaviors'.

Expanding on the above definitions are the explanations that follow;

Primary

It is primary because it is an entity in itself and not caused by other factors. A bit of a what-came-first-the-chicken-or-the-egg dilemma. This can be a difficult concept for many to understand. Although the complexity of addiction and mental health means that there are no exact answers for a person's addiction (it is a combination of things), I would like to clarify what the primary part of this description gives rise to. Firstly, being primary means it is the cause of, and not the result of; this means that a person doesn't have depression and therefore drinks, it means that a person has depression because he/she drinks.

Another example is that of the diagnosis of bipolar, (I'm not a doctor so have no authority on which to make such diagnosis, and in some cases, the diagnosis is spot on), however. I see many people with this diagnosis and it is only true because of their addiction. What do I mean by that? If they stop the drinking and drugging, the bipolar problem goes away.

Putting 'primary' in a social context, we end up with having to challenge a few ideas that people have around why they drink or drug. I hear often 'I drink / drug because my life is a mess.' No, your life is a mess because you drink or drug! 'I drink because my wife left me.' No, your wife left you because you drink. And finally, 'I smoke weed because I can't get a job.' No, you can't get a job because you smoke weed. I think you get the message.

I am not saying that the primary diagnosis is the right one all the time. Some people are genuinely ill or have had disastrous relationships or can't get work.

Chronic

It is chronic because a client cannot return to 'normal' substance use once an addiction is established. Once you've got it you've got it. Many people will argue against this and advocate such things such as controlled drinking. This may be possible with some people. Generally, once someone's addiction has reached the point of neuro-adaption then there is little chance of returning to a pre-state where the addiction does not become all-consuming if they pick up again. In my experience, addiction is like any other chronic illness such as heart disease or diabetes. Once I've got it, then I need to do something about it on daily basis. It is a long-lasting condition that can be controlled, not cured. For me, that includes all the elements of a biopsychosocial model.

Progressive

It is progressive because symptoms and consequences continue to occur with increasing severity as use continues. In the words of AA, it gets worse never better. There is no doubt that as addiction progresses along a timeline then other conditions get worse. Apart from the obvious changes in tolerance and dependency, there are also increased physiological diseases that we all know about;

liver disease, pancreatitis, and multiple cancers, to name but a few.

Under the ASAM definition there are further headings that I relate to and believe are absolutely real.

Brain reward

Many aspects of a disease state are reflected in the idea of brain reward, not only in the physiological sense but also in behavior and emotional. Addiction affects neurotransmitters and reward structures in the brain. We can't argue this and as science progresses we are able to examine the brain in finer detail to see what is happening during addiction. The parts of the brain, which are connected to reward circuitry, motivation and memory are not functioning as they should, leading to the obvious problems associated with addiction. So, when people take a drink or use drugs, a chain reaction happens in the brain that stimulates the reward pathways leading to feelings of pleasure and joy. Various receptors are at play, in particular, dopamine, and we feel so good or euphoric that an incredibly powerful association is formed that leads people to want to use their drug of choice again. We are defenceless against that process. How does that look in behavior and emotion? Somehow, the thought of taking a drink or drug seems more exciting than the consequences and people will use again despite all evidence to the contrary. Willpower has been short-circuited and choice has disappeared.

Motivation

Obviously, motivation is affected by the brain circuitry as mentioned above. Looking at the behaviors and emotions, we see people apply levels of motivation that are incredible and can be baffling to many. Despite all that may have gone wrong in a person's active addiction, a level of illogical motivation can kick in that leads a person to break all sorts of personal boundaries, break rules, drive cars, jump out of windows, and generally seek their drug of choice with a motivation that is incredibly powerful. AA members have for years recognised that during active addiction the motivation to carry on drinking is almost an unstoppable force in its own right.

Memory

Again, brain circuitry is affected by drugs or alcohol. Alcohol is, in particular, a depressant that acts on all the central nervous system and as such leads to impairment in memory encoding. There are also various other effects of long-term alcohol use that will lead to memory loss. For instance, because of long-term alcohol use, the brain will be deficient in the B vitamin thiamine. This can lead to a condition known as Korsakoff's Syndrome that has fatal and irreversible consequences if not treated. Amnesia is common with the syndrome that presents similarly to dementia.

People with addiction issues can relate to periods of memory loss ranging from a couple of minutes to hours or even months. On the flip side of this, no matter how strong memories may be of someone's last disaster with drugs or alcohol, those memories may not be strong enough to stop them drinking again.

Biological

Biological changes in the body and brain are well documented. When we understand these, we can see how human biology programmes us to pursue and repeat pleasurable experiences. Further to this is the physiology of each person, their genetics, and brain function, which all have a part to play in their addiction and are influential on a person's propensity to addiction. It is possible to have no predisposition to addiction at all and still get addicted. Again, chicken-and-egg stuff and an area often debated. We also see the development of tolerance and dependency as just some of the obvious biological changes within the body.

Psychological

Cognitive distortions are a main part of this book and how they manifest in addiction. You will read plenty more of this as you progress. For this section, though, I shall keep it brief. There is no doubt that people with addictions have multiple problems of varying degrees when dealing with feelings, emotions, thinking, and making choices. Again, this is well documented but I wanted to add some of the mental twists that go with addiction. In Twelve-Step recovery, picking up that drink or drug again, despite all the evidence it will go wrong, is considered a form of insanity. You will hear of many ways in which the illness psychologically manifests. A bizarre one that comes to mind is that of hiding bottles of booze around the house. This sounds fairly logical if you don't want people to find your supply but then why is it common for people who live on their own to carry out the same behavior? I hear of this often. Perhaps it is connected with the shame or guilt, I hear you cry, and it may be so, but if you live in isolation why the need?

Social

There are many characteristic social aspects of addiction. Relationships suffer, and people neglect responsibilities at home, work, or school. The alcoholic withdraws mentally from any intimacy and responsibility within relationships and forms an inability to relate to family and community. Financial difficulties arise, perhaps leading to legal problems and crime and then, of course, there can be employment issues. Bad judgements can be made in regards to long-term consequences and the addict is indeed in all sorts of social difficulty.

Spiritual

I am sure that, so far, nearly everyone can relate to or understand (even if you don't agree) all that has been written. But how is the spiritual aspect explained? Especially for some as they refuse to acknowledge its existence. ASAM describes this area as 'Distortions in meaning, purpose and values that guide attitudes, thinking and behavior' as well as 'Distortions in a person's connection with self, with others and with the transcendent (referred to as God by many, the Higher Power by Twelve-Steps groups, or higher consciousness by others).' We live in a secular society, especially in the UK and especially when it comes to drug and alcohol treatment. There are many people very angry about the use of the God word and the mention of any church attendance or spiritual connection. To me, I find this attitude a little disingenuous and certainly damaging to a person's recovery when we consider that this anti-spiritual element can be strongly put across by professionals working in the field of recovery. It frustrates me that professionals are meant to have a person-centred attitude, putting aside their personal feelings and biases about their clients yet when it comes spiritual discussions, the barriers come down and attitudes rear up aplenty; sometimes to the point of shaming people for their spiritual beliefs. I am sure that many professionals who only believe in medication-assisted recovery attend weddings and christenings in churches quite often.

Why else is the spiritual element so important to people? AA talks about spiritual awakenings and spiritual experiences. Two different things. The spiritual experience being of a life-changing, supernatural event that leads someone to have an overwhelming 'God' experience that is followed by a vast change in feelings and outlook. A spiritual awakening is a slow process where someone finds themselves changing over a period of time. This happens through education and with determination and dedication. Sometimes, others see this change in a person before they do but all agree that the profound alteration in a person's reactions to life is fundamentally different from what they once were.

So why is it so important? People recount how they realised that they were living in spiritual darkness, a spiritual void, where they felt lonely, unloved, miserable and out of touch with anything nice. People tell tales of always feeling as if they were surrounded by doom, it was a dark and tangible presence all around them. Once they found recovery, the darkness went. They felt joy and love again, no longer felt isolated, and could laugh without fear. To me, these are the real joys of a person finding a new life and having a spiritual awakening.

Introduction

An Introduction to CBT and the Twelve Steps

Definitions of the models

What is CBT?

In simple terms CBT, (Cognitive Behavioral Therapy), is a talking-and-action therapy that can help a person manage their problems by changing the way they think and behave. It is an action-oriented form of psychosocial therapy that assumes that faulty thinking patterns cause negative behavior and emotions

It looks at why people think and behave in the way they do and then gives them options that result in change. The treatment focuses on changing an individual's thoughts in order to change his or her behavior and emotional state.

CBT also recognises the importance of support groups, which, as we know, are mostly in the format of self-help groups such as AA. In these groups, people can learn from each other, support each other, become part of a social network and 'vent' emotion, fears, and pain in a 'safe environment'. CBT recommends setting up group rules and most Twelve-Step meetings will follow a format that people are generally expected to adhere to. This doesn't always work but people are mostly welcomed back. AA meetings have a yellow card on which is written 'Who you see here, what you hear here, when you leave here, let it stay here' and, likewise, CBT groups have an understanding of the need for confidentiality.

What are the Twelve Steps?

The Twelve Steps are a set of guiding principles outlining a course of action for recovery from addiction, compulsion, or other behavioral problems. The Steps focus on changing an individual's thoughts in order to change his or her behavior and emotional state. The Twelve Steps do not require the individual to hold particular religious beliefs, nor spiritual or secular views. The individual is free to believe, or not believe, anything they wish.

One of the unique and wonderful things about Twelve-Step meetings is the breakthroughs people have when they have been living in shame of their condition. They may have been hiding aspects of themselves that they were afraid to share. Feeling isolated, lonely, and stupid they kept their problems hidden from others in case others found out what they were really like or really thinking. When a person attends fellowship meetings (they have to go to more than one) then they find a large group of people, worldwide, who have all had the same or similar thoughts, behaviors, and shame. The person no longer has to conceal who they are and how they feel. People often share things in fellowship meetings that outside of the meeting ordinary folk would think insane, odd, crazy, or extremely funny. Inside the meeting, everyone just nods their heads in knowing agreement. This is extremely therapeutic for the person.

Simple doesn't mean easy

Many a time in recovery meetings, people will hear the phrase 'It's a simple programme'; this doesn't mean it's easy. If it was we'd have fewer alcoholics and addicts in the world. No, easy it isn't. Any therapy, whether it be CBT or Twelve Steps requires personal effort; a lot of personal effort. A person may need to swallow their pride, time and time again, in order to achieve long-term sobriety. That level of determination is certainly not easy to maintain, especially with all the emotional turmoil of early recovery. People may feel as if they have gone back to school having to learn things through repetition, will find themselves at a loss as to what people are talking about –both CBT and the Twelve Steps use their own language, which will take a while to learn – and any person will get frustrated; often wanting to have twelve months of sobriety in six weeks. Perseverance is a must.

Why do they work?

Both approaches work by changing people's attitudes and their behavior by focusing on the thoughts, images, beliefs, and attitudes that influence their behavior and lead them to self-destructive actions. The two approaches within CBT that really resonate with Twelve-Step recovery are the behavioral and the cognitive.

The behavioral approach is very applicable to Twelve-Step recovery. It is very practical to change behaviors by educating people on safe behaviors or dangerous behaviors. In CBT, a therapist may challenge peoples' unsafe behaviors and in Twelve-Step meetings, people will learn things like 'take a different route home' and 'avoid wet places'. Both give rise to new behavior and avoidance of trigger situations.

The cognitive approach is also applicable to Twelve-Step recovery. Often, a person's understanding of the world and his or her own behavior, are based on an incorrect belief system. The 'Big Book' of AA, *Alcoholics Anonymous*, says that at the end of a person's drinking, they cannot 'differentiate the true from the false'. These incorrect systems hinder their ability to love themselves or others, can lead to blame and resentment, and can keep other people away.

Both approaches are helping people to learn new skills of self-management that they will then put into practice in everyday life. In Twelve-Step meetings, people will learn things like 'I'm not responsible for my first thought', meaning that people learn not to react to the first things that pop into their heads. They read and hear slogans like 'one day at a time', 'keep it simple', 'live and let live', and 'don't pick up the first drink and you can't get drunk'. All these new ways of thinking help to reduce the internal voices that can keep a person repeating old behaviors.

The role of CBT and the Twelve Steps is to allow people to choose between helpful and unhelpful patterns and behaviors. Neither is about programming people to follow one set of behaviors. They are about letting people choose and rise above their own previous conditioning. In the fellowships, people share their experiences, strengths, and hopes; they do not give advice or dictate. Freedom from addiction is not really free if someone is being made to do it.

Other Important Areas

Positive selfishness

It is often heard in fellowship meetings that the Twelve Steps are a selfish programme. There can be some confusion around this and a lack of understanding. CBT considers **positive** selfishness as a useful mindset. A person can be helped to understand the importance of this; learning to put themselves first. This has to be done with an awareness of what positive selfishness means.

It is not alright for a person to selfishly take from others in order to please oneself without giving back. So, positive selfishness is a state that sees a person getting well and then becoming able to perform at their best. This leads to things like, being there for others and being able to live a balanced, healthy productive life. If these things are not achieved then most people are likely to fall apart and be unable to cope.

There is nothing more important to realise, in a person's early recovery from addiction, than this – if a person does not focus on recovery, does not attend appointments, puts relationships first, or a job, or a holiday then that person is unlikely to find stable enough ground to maintain their recovery. It will all come tumbling down. This is often learned through bitter experience.

Someone who is **negatively** selfish deliberately puts them self before others to the point where others are injured, hurt, or left in detrimental situations. This person could be an abuser or manipulator, using their own strengths to force others into a point of submission or cooperation.

Factors enabling progress

Considered one of the fathers of modern psychological theories, Carl Rogers has influenced modern psychotherapy and has directly impacted the field of mental health at great depth. He identified six factors necessary for psychological growth and suggested that when these conditions are met, a person will move towards a constructive fulfilment of potential. I see these at work within the Twelve-Step arena and so strongly that, perhaps, non-Twelve-Step services find the relationships in Twelve-Step recovery overwhelming, overly friendly, and threatening. According to Rogerian theory, the six factors necessary for growth are:

1. Therapist-client psychological contact:

This first condition simply states that a relationship between therapist and client must exist in order for the client to achieve positive personal change. Within Twelve-Step meetings, these relationships are strong and dependable. Sponsor and sponsee will have a trusting relationship and bond that is rarely seen outside of the self-help culture. The following five factors are characteristics of the therapist-client relationship, and they may vary by degree. I'm not saying that Twelve-Step meetings are therapy and that sponsors are therapists, just that these factors exist strongly within the Twelve-Step environment.

2. Client incongruence or vulnerability:

A discrepancy between the client's self-image and actual experience leaves him or her vulnerable to fears and anxieties. The client is often unaware of the incongruence. To explain this a little further, imagine that when you were a small child you wanted to be a dancer, firefighter, or movie star. You may have achieved those things, or none of them, but certainly ended up with an addiction problem that then makes these dreams out of reach. Even if you are a firefighter you know you could be a better one if it wasn't for your addiction. So, you are left with frustration, stress and anxiety about your impossible dream. You have learned the pain of incongruence.

3. *Therapist congruence or genuineness:*

The therapist should be self-aware, genuine, and congruent. This does not imply that the therapist be a picture of perfection but that he or she be true to him- or herself within the therapeutic relationship. Often, when people go to their first few meetings, they are astonished by the levels of honesty and genuineness at which people share. They have never come across people that are so willing to be completely honest about stuff that, not only can they relate to, but had no idea others had felt or done apart from them self.

4. *Therapist unconditional positive regard:*

The clients' experiences, positive or negative, should be accepted by the therapist without any conditions or judgement. In this way, the client can share experiences without fear of being judged. In fellowship meetings, the unconditional positive regard is abundant. People from all walks of life are made to feel welcome, given a coffee, shown to a seat and are given a hand to shake or a shown a warm and friendly smile.

5. Therapist empathy:

The therapist demonstrates empathic understanding of the clients' experiences and recognises emotional experiences without getting emotionally involved. The newcomer at meetings soon starts to realise that people know what they are talking about, have been through, and have experienced their feelings. The empathy is a real one, does not feel rehearsed or forced, and is not learned out of a book.

6. Client perception:

To some degree, the client perceives the therapist's unconditional positive regard and empathic understanding. This is communicated through the words and behaviors of the therapist. Again, in Twelve-Step meetings people perceive this easy and unforced understanding of the others at the meeting. They feel at home and that people at the meeting are genuine and caring. This sometimes goes against all their preconceived ideas of what AA is about.

Examples in this book

Some of the examples may seem petty or trite and you may not even believe them, (unless you have attended a fair few fellowship meetings). Please, let me reassure you they are genuine and powerful for the persons concerned. (No names are used.) Just because you're scared of spiders and I'm not doesn't make the fear any less real for you.

It's all in the words

Part of my goal in writing this book is to get across the point that we are all talking the same talk but are using different words to do so. The CBT approach talks about 'cognitive distortions' while AA is talking about 'stinking thinking'. When CBT talks about thinking errors, AA refers to 'isms' (more on isms later).

Therapists are put off by words such as 'God', 'higher power', and spiritual awakening. AA members are put off by words and phrases like 'disputational methods', 'collaborative empiricism', and 'ego deflation'

Cut the legs off the bed

So, what is it about these practical models that has been so successful for millions? Why do these approaches resonate so well with some and not others? Our individual differences, personalities, need for answers, faith, and all those multitudes of difference make some models work for some and not others. As a therapist, it is not my role to decide which one is best for me and my beliefs but what is best for my clients and theirs. The practical approach of the Steps and CBT can be explained in this teaching story.

A person had been seeing a therapist for months. He spent time lying on the couch, or sitting in the comfy chair talking about childhood, family history, all sort of pains and woes but still had the problem of not sleeping at night due to the monsters under his bed. One day, he doesn't return for his overly expensive sessions. The therapist bumps into him a year later and asks if he is OK. He says he has never been better.

'But what about the monsters under the bed?' the therapist asks.

'Oh, no problem,' says the client, 'I went to see a CBT therapist.'

'Wow, what happened to make the monsters go away?' she asks.

'Simple,' he said. 'The therapist just told me to cut the legs off the bed.'

What's the point I'm trying to make? We are all different and need different solutions. Some people will really benefit from the analytical approach and would be horrified if expected to do otherwise. Some people need action and direction. We are all incredibly complex, as are the reasons for addiction. There is no one-box-fits-all solution. I've read of highly respected doctors and professionals who say the only reason for addiction is trauma, others that say it is all down to brain chemistry and others yet, that say the only relevance is the role society plays in a person's life. Some say it's the drug that causes addiction and some say it isn't. It's all of those things and we are sure of one outcome – addiction is an epidemic. It is so destructive and cunning that the whole world is in denial about its impact. Look up the facts and figures: in 2016, the USA numbers for drug deaths were around 59,000 and around 88,000 for alcohol, and they are only the ones that are reported. We know multiple occasions were an alcohol-related death is recorded as something else entirely; a head injury, liver failure, car crash, etc. It's appalling.

Sponsor-sponsee or parent-child?

Touching on the Transactional Analysis model of parent-adult-child, I want to briefly discuss sponsorship as I see it relating to this model.

In early recovery, I see the relationship as one of parent-child.

The sponsor is the Parent. Traditionally in this model, this means that the 'parent' persona is made up of the behaviors thoughts and feelings of our parents, or other parental figures. A person learns things like 'don't steal', 'don't lie', 'don't forget', or 'always do this and never do that'. Similarly, the 'parent' role of the sponsor has been learned from his or her sponsor. And the sponsee (child) hears things like, 'don't pick up the first drink and you can't get drunk', 'avoid wet places', 'a day at a time' and many other rules that will help maintain sobriety and thus recovery.

We can split the 'parent' into two further states: 1. The Critical Parent who is corrective and prohibitive and 2. The Nurturing Parent who is affirming and gentle in the guidance they give. Sponsors may fall into either one of these categories, or both if they are skilled and experienced enough.

The sponsee is the 'child'. Traditionally in this model, that means that the child will respond to instruction or poor evaluation by looking at the floor, crying, getting angry or stamping feet. This has similarities to early recovery when the person is resistant to their counsellor or sponsor, takes offence at learning the truth or facing up to negative behaviors, and is slightly resentful in peaks and troughs towards the leading figure. Sometimes, a person feels they are being forced into the child role and feels that this is unjust and unwarranted. They feel patronised (literally) and belittled.

The Adult persona is the person who keeps the 'parent' and 'child' in balance. This is the state that both the sponsor and sponsee should be striving for. The relationship should end up equal with both parties being able to listen attentively to each other and not be defensive nor threatening. Conversations should be more along the line of problem-solving as equals.

Chapter One

Step One

'We admitted we were powerless over alcohol / our addiction, that our lives had become unmanageable.'

Defining the problem

Both in CBT and the Twelve Steps, defining the problem is a common starting point. Bill Wilson, in the early 1930s, had learned the first part from Dr Silkworth, and that was that he had a disease with both mental and physical elements. Secondly, that he had to have a fundamental change in his thinking and actions that could only come from believing in something other than himself, whatever that may be. Bill had discovered the two core principles on which AA was built. Firstly, a person had to admit to the problem (Step One) and secondly, they had to open up to a solution.

CBT has a common expression that the 'solution is the problem' and reinforces the need to be able to assess your problems and recognise that your current coping strategies are part of that problem. The problem behaviors associated with addiction and the repeated return to the drug of choice seem to the addict to be the only solution to the problems. The fact is that these coping strategies and behaviors are the cause of the problem. It is often a shock for someone who repeatedly says, 'I drink because my wife left me' to find out his wife left him because he drinks. Likewise, the weed smoker who says he smokes because he can't find a job is probably jobless because he smokes weed regularly. Finally, the person who says she drinks because of depression will often find that this is the other way around, she is depressed because she drinks. This fits in with the ASAM definition that recognises addiction as a primary illness – it is the cause of many problems not the result of them. Of course, this isn't to say that there aren't genuine mental-health issues and that some people's lives aren't so difficult that they use drugs and alcohol to cope.

So why are the two approaches linked? Both strategies recognise that the short-term fix is not working and that it is indeed counterproductive. Step One identifies this in the admission of powerlessness and unmanageability and CBT recognises this in the need to identify and define the problem.

Mental obsession – active addiction

In early recovery and active addiction, the mental obsession with drugs and alcohol is incredibly powerful. A person may not be able to think about anything else other than booze or drugs. To the non-addict, this may be hard to grasp. It's a bit like buying a yellow car and then seeing hundreds of them. Up until then, you thought no one else had one. The alcoholic will see booze everywhere. Walking into a shop will be torture. There is alcohol everywhere: it is on the TV, on posters, the sides of buses, and all over the sports channel. It can be completely overwhelming. Many a newcomer when questioned will confess to having thoughts along the lines of, 'Don't think about alcohol, don't think about alcohol'. It makes no kind of sense to others. For starters, telling yourself not to think about alcohol **is** thinking about alcohol, and, secondly, non-addicts can't understand why a person would be holding onto thoughts of something that has been so destructive in their lives. Believe me, it is unintentional and it will go away.

There are many references in AA's book *Alcoholics Anonymous* to obsessional thinking. Fred and Jim's stories about their lack of judgement when it came to ordering drinks after a period of sobriety, the great obsession of every abnormal drinker to one day control and enjoy his drinking, and the feelings of being restless, irritable, and discontent all contribute to the overall picture of obsessional thinking when it comes to drugs and alcohol.

CBT refers to obsessional thinking as persistent

- Unwanted thoughts

- Images

- Doubts

- Urges

- Compulsions

When these areas become significantly distressful and sufficient enough to interfere with your life then they have become a problem. Add drugs or alcohol into the mix and we are back to Bill Wilson discovering that addiction is a disease with both mental and physical elements. People develop tolerance and dependency as a normal physical response to their drug of choice and this, combined with the mental preoccupation that occurs during addiction, leaves a person with what AA refers to as a mental obsession. This leads to people becoming powerless over their drug of choice.

Powerless

I read and hear controversy around the word 'powerless' all the time. Certain recovery movements fight it with a vengeance. I can only share from my own experience and that of those close to me. Admitting to being powerless over alcohol has been the touchstone of many peoples' recovery. It does not, however, mean that people are powerless over everything, are a pushover, or can't make decisions for themselves. Indeed, in my experience, this leads a person to become strongly independent, a competent decision maker and a leader in many circles, able to speak confidently in front of groups of people. How many employees don't know that their director, chief exec or manager is in Twelve-Step recovery?

In regards to CBT, the word powerless connects with helplessness, which is a core belief that links with a lack of control, weakness, and feelings of being trapped with no way out. This is, indeed, how people feel about their addiction with a really strong belief that they will never be able to change a thing. Often, people who believe they are helpless have difficulty making a change. Feeling helpless in one area may lead a person to be overly controlling in another and, again, this is something common to addiction with many people overcompensating in certain areas of their lives to make up for the hidden and painful elements.

Unmanageable

It's incredible to realise that the process of being unmanageable becomes a driver to continue an addiction. This is explained in numerous ways as the book continues. Starting simply, people may talk about being unmanageable in several ways. A person can be late to work every day, forget to pay the bills, or miss appointments. Although the initial problems come from a place of unmanageability it can all soon become much more and can develop into strong emotional problems and fear. Fear to go to work, after being late, in case the boss finds you out. Fear to open the letter that just arrived in case it's the bill from last month you forgot to pay and you fear that you're in trouble. Fear that it's the letter from the benefits office stopping your payments because you missed the appointment. The list goes on.

CBT can help people make sense of all the confusion that seems to be going on, bringing manageability to the way people have overcomplicated things. Over complication is another way of unmanageability presenting itself.

Below are some indicators of overcomplicating things, not all of them so obvious:

- Messy and cluttered personal and workspaces.

- Overcomplicating methods and behaviors.

- Completely unmanageable timekeeping,

  - Lateness

  - Overly booked timetables

  - Wasting time people-pleasing

  - Unimportant stuff taking up the day

- Micro-managing can be a form of unmanageability. The anxiety developed around not letting others do it their way can be quite overpowering.

- Unmanageability of feelings, for instance, falling in love with the first person who says hello.

- Not being able to say what you mean; giving overly complicated explanations.

A great example of overcomplicating things to the point they become unmanageable is that of cooking a meal. Instead of sticking to the recipe and following the simple rules, a person decides they know best and starts to add more – and more – until the meal becomes a big mess that is not edible to anyone. Try making a meringue without following the instructions!

Post-Acute Withdrawal Syndrome

An area of importance, when considering those early days of recovery, is one known as Post-Acute Withdrawal Syndrome (PAWS). This complex and difficult stage of a person's recovery can last for a long time. Starting with acute withdrawal, or the first stage, we see a person suffering some, or all of these symptoms and is important to recognise that some will definitely need medical support from a doctor who prescribes the right medication. Let a doctor make that decision.

Including these lists in Step One may seem of no relevance to some and I apologise for adding them formatted as a list. They are however very appropriate and the signs and symptoms listed can have a great impact on early recovery. AA has a fantastic world network telephone service that responds to peoples' calls twenty-four hours a day, 365 days a year. The result of that call may mean that someone pays a visit to the individual who made the call and takes them to a meeting (at that person's request). This can be a good thing, as far as reaching out for help and engaging in recovery activities. Often when a person is feeling sick and tired of being sick and tired then their motivation to engage is high. As it says in the 'big book' it may be worth waiting until he (the newcomer or prospect) returns from a binge before engaging.

Second to this, is a reminder to people that those first few days are a pretty hazardous place to be. People do die in withdrawal and particularly from alcohol.

The mild physical symptoms of acute withdrawal will start fairly quickly and can last anywhere between twelve to thirty-six hours. The symptoms include the following:

- Insomnia, restlessness
- Fast heart rate
- Sweating, facial flushing
- Muscle trembling or spasms
- Numbness, tingling, or burning sensations in the arms or legs
- Nausea, vomiting
- Ringing in the ears
- Dry mouth
- Itching
- Anxiety
- Paranoia

The severe physical symptoms of acute withdrawal will start fairly quickly and can last anywhere between five hours and three days. The symptoms include:

- Seizures
- Chest infections
- Severe pain in the stomach
- Poor balance when walking
- Hand and body tremors
- Hallucinations
- Paranoia – worsening
- Confusion

In PAWS, or second stage, there are a whole host of other difficulties going on. These symptoms can last up to six months and do recur in some individuals.

- Insomnia, restlessness
- Headache
- Tiredness, weakness
- Muscle trembles
- Sexual problems
- Stomach pain
- Anxiety
- Depression, mood swings
- Irritability
- Poor concentration

- Poor memory
- Impulsiveness
- Difficulty in thinking clearly, making plans or decisions
- Disturbed sleep

With all this going on then, those first six months are, again, a rough ride for someone. They will certainly feel powerless and unmanageable but here, I think, is an important part: when a person has completed, or attempted to complete, the Twelve Steps in those early days they may have not been very good at it. Their brains are giving them a hard time and they are really struggling to learn and engage and, in my opinion, revisiting the Steps is vital for long-term recovery. I often hear of people in Twelve-Step fellowships reviewing their progress, talking about how the steps apply to them now, and how their ideas have changed. There are also those who recognise that Step Ten is about revisiting all the Steps on a daily basis. 'Crikey, that's a bit much,' I hear you say. It soon becomes an enjoyable routine that is no longer the burden that people perceive.

Long-term issues

It is important for newcomers to recovery to understand that just taking away the drink or drugs is not the complete solution. There are many other issues and problems a person will have to deal with that make those early months, or even years, hard work.

Mood swings

Mood swings can last several months, are sometimes baffling, and can seemingly arise from nowhere. Understanding that this is a part of the recovery journey can be of help to some. It is important to remember that if people with dependency issues don't give their doctor the full picture, i.e. 'I'm early in recovery', then a false diagnosis can be made. This is not the doctor's fault; it's difficult to diagnose properly without the full picture. Often the denial around addiction extends to what truths people tell their physician so diagnoses end up being made that include anxiety, bipolar, or depression.

Insomnia

Insomnia can be common in early recovery, lasting several months. It is a difficult stage people will have to go through. Medication to assist sleep is a controversial area but putting in place routines and behaviors that can help is recommended.

Here is a top-ten list of common sleep advice.

1. Turn off TVs, computers, mobile phones, or tablets an hour before going to bed. The blue light they emit is associated with sleeplessness. Letting your thoughts relax and prepare for sleep is not aided when engaged with these machines.

2. Avoid daytime naps. If tired during the day try to engage in something to keep you active rather than napping.

3. Your bedroom should be for sleeping (mostly). Having a TV or working in bed / surfing the net does not make for a relaxing atmosphere.

4. Try to get some routine. Get up and go to bed at the same time. Your body gets used to the routine.

5. Stop looking at your clock/phone/tablet because you'll only find things to worry about or get engaged in, not good for sleep.

6. Avoid caffeine.

7. If, in recovery, you have found you now enjoy exercise, then try to time it so you have a gap of about three hours before bed after a workout.

8. Don't eat too late.

9. If you keep getting up for trips to the bathroom then cut down on fluid intake prior to bed.

10. Remember, smoking can make sleeping harder.

Drinking/Using dreams

Often unheard of outside of the addiction arena, is the topic of drinking dreams. I have heard many people, some in long-term recovery (multiple years), talking about drinking or using dreams. They are incredibly powerful and usually revolve around someone's drug of choice. The dream may or may not include use of the substance, but the feelings of anxiety the dream can give rise to are certainly real. A person may wake from the dream in a cold sweat utterly convinced it has all gone wrong and that they have or will use again and have a feeling of 'what's the point?' Thanks, subconscious mind. Understanding a person's dreams has value in the fact that it may lead to deeper understanding of one's fears and anxieties and maybe the things that have been running around in their subconscious that are causing the person the issues for which they present. In the case of drinking, or using, dreams, there seems to be an obvious connection to the angst around those days of using, which manifests itself in dreams that are full of fear, cause internal conflict, and are downright scary. People can wake from these dreams feeling guilt and anxiety. They can sometimes take a while to realise that the dream was not real and that they did not relapse. This is powerful stuff and people should recognise the impact these dreams may have on someone in recovery. Emotional hangovers are mentioned in the Twelve Steps and the feelings a person gets after one of these dreams could fall into this category.

After many, many, years of studying dreams, there is still no good system of working out what they mean. There are, however, definite connections to the cognitive state of a person. For instance, people with PTSD have more nightmares than others, as do those going through periods of emotional stress. Even though we can't make the direct links to the symbolism of the context in dreams, we can make a direct link to the distress they can cause. Waking after a bad dream can leave people feeling upset and anxious. They may have feelings of impending doom or feel bad about themselves. Whichever it is, CBT recognises the importance of that connection and, more importantly, addressing the thoughts a person has about themselves as a result of those dreams.

Mental obsession – Recovery

Mental obsession with a drug of choice can be a long-term issue and it is covered in detail earlier in this chapter. One further element to add in this section is the point that people can often find themselves having an odd relationship with their drug of choice. It is not uncommon for someone with multiple years of recovery to mention that they had recently been mesmerised by someone drinking alcohol in a restaurant (or such a place) that they were in. They felt utterly unable to understand how a person made a glass of wine last several hours, and then that person left some of it in the glass.

Emotional immaturity

Emotional immaturity is an important area to consider for persons trying to get well. I often hear people speak of getting into recovery but having the emotional maturity of the teenager they were when they started drinking. What is the truth behind this? Is it an excuse for bad behavior or is there a grain of truth? Certainly, people will have cognitive distortions and unstable emotions that with practice can mature and become steady and manageable. According to several sources, the connection is real with people having difficulty coping with life challenges; they are more likely to suffer from stress, have low self-esteem, have unrealistic expectations and find self-control difficult. Emotional immaturity can be a real problem for recovery, as mentioned before; recovery is not just about putting down the drink or drug, it is about the living and coping afterwards.

Step One conclusion

It can take between three months and a year (longer in some cases) to fully recover from the effects of alcohol or drugs. Even then, the brain remains abnormally sensitive to alcohol or drugs. If a person starts drinking again, the high tolerance that their body has developed can come back within a few days. It's why doctors usually recommend that a person doesn't start drinking again, even in moderation.

In Step One we compare the admission of powerlessness to the obsessional thoughts, compulsions, and doubts that CBT recognises. The unmanageability compares to the manifestation of over-complication that is broken down in CBT. We recognise the complications of withdrawing from drugs or alcohol that lead to the short and long-term effects on every aspect of recovery and in particular the effect that will have on a person's ability to be emotionally stable and operate at their full learning capacity.

Chapter Two
Step Two

'Came to believe that a Power greater than ourselves could restore us to sanity.'

Change

This Step is all about change. For change to take place, a person needs to realise where they are, what is their current position or status, and how they are functioning in the world. Are they having any problems or not? Further on in this chapter, there is a section on denial, which is a powerful enemy of the alcoholic. Denial will battle with the need for change and will throw up all sorts of barriers to getting well. Many a time, a person will go to an AA meeting, enter treatment, or have a detox and still believe there is nothing wrong. 'I'm just not like them' or 'It's OK, I've got this under control' will be heard often and, perhaps, to the point of frustration from loved ones. I am a firm believer that if someone has, reluctantly, gone to an AA meeting or to a treatment provider then *something* must be wrong, something definitely needs to change.

CBT looks at the idea that the way you see the world, including yourself, affects your thoughts and feelings, and if those are particularly negative they will lead to mental health problems. In order to move away from those problems, a person must change the way they think and, if they change the way that they think, then they will change their mental health.

In the next chapter, there is a focus on finding out those things that may reinforce the need for change.

Step over to the bar – experiments and evidence

There is an experiment in the book *Alcoholics Anonymous* that is about clarifying a person's addiction to alcohol. It reads like this: 'Step over to the nearest barroom and try some controlled drinking. Try to drink and stop abruptly. Try it more than once...It may be worth a bad case of the jitters if you get full knowledge of your condition.' This experiment is a practical exercise that will challenge a person's beliefs about themselves. If they are completely honest and are able to be honest, then they will learn a great deal.

CBT also advocates for experimenting. Behavioral experiments are planned activities that use observation or experimentation, both in session or in between. They help people check out the validity of thoughts, ideas, or behaviors. People can then work out what works for them or not. When they recognise that how they think about things influences how they feel about them they are starting to take steps forward. Completing mind maps, thought sheets, or diaries are supportive in helping people to identify patterns of behavior, but for people to be fully convinced that change is possible or that alternatives to their thinking can be achieved then they may need to take practical action. Action is the key word of Twelve-Step recovery and CBT.

Came, came to, came to believe

The Twelve-Step approach can be seen as a series of experiments. Firstly, a person may not believe they are alcoholic and they might attend meetings just to listen, find out more information and confirm, or dismiss, their ideas about themselves. In meetings, people hear new ideas or ways of handling situations or old behaviors. They will attempt them in their own time, maybe without telling people they are doing so. In the early days, people will be reluctant to talk, may feel that what they have to say is invalid or petty and are full of fear about sharing their thoughts. AA meetings will guide them through this process. Through various ways, people will start to talk more, whether it be reading out the pre-amble or serving teas and coffees. They will find their voice more. Each time they talk, they move away from the anxiety that they first felt. The experiment is working. In between meetings, people will try out the ideas they have heard or been told. They find out that, although it may be awful, they can stay away from a drink or drug one day at a time, that this then can add up to two days, and before long they've chalked up a week or more. They are amazed that the experiment worked. Even if a person relapses they now have evidence that they can stay sober for periods of time, and with the right support will be able to build on this. A great CBT saying is that there is no such thing as failure, only feedback. Second to this, as anyone who reads Twelve Step literature will know, *Came to Believe* is a popular book that is about the emerging spiritual awareness that people go through with regards a higher power. It is a useful piece of writing that will help most find an understanding that there is a difference between being spiritual and being religious.

Seeking evidence

Further to the above ideas, seeking evidence can be a key part of breaking the cycle of denial. Whether that denial is around drink or drug use or behaviors and thoughts, once a person starts to believe the evidence (they may not believe it) then the possibilities of change start to happen. A person can see where they are now and envisage where they want to be.

ABC

The ABC approach is the first and main method of thought identification in CBT. It is used to match thoughts to feelings and events (not always in that order). Using this approach helps a person to identify and challenge the irrational or troublesome thoughts that lead to negative outcomes. It is as follows:

Activating event

A – This is the situation or event that ultimately leads to some type of high emotional response or negative dysfunctional thinking. Often referred to in treatment services as a trigger event that may lead to relapse or crisis. It may be worth noting that some persons often express that they have no idea what the event was, they just thought it would be a good idea to pick up a drink. These events that lead up to a relapse are commonly talked about within the Twelve-Step approach.

Belief

B – Beliefs. In the second column, the client writes down the negative thoughts that occurred to them. For instance, 'I could have done better. I'm a failure.'

Consequences

C – Consequence. The third column is for the negative feelings and dysfunctional behaviors that ensued. The negative thoughts in the second column are seen as a connecting bridge between the situation and the distressing feelings. The third column, C, is next explained by describing emotions or negative thoughts that the client thinks are caused by A. This could be anger, sorrow, anxiety, etc.

Sanity

A strong word that scares people and sends them into a state of rebellion against the Twelve Steps. This word is too much for some people. By using the word 'sanity', the Twelve Steps must be implying that there is a level of 'insanity' and I'm afraid this is indeed the case. When people focus hard on the things that they have done, the decisions they have made, the risks they took, or the stuff they swallowed, then, if honest, there is some really insane history to their life that perhaps they don't want others to know. Even if some of the things they did were just slightly illogical or were errors in judgement the 'sanity' of it all is worth exploring.

Core beliefs

Many people have learned negative core beliefs. As a form of insanity, they fuel negative perceptions of oneself that have become delusional; that is to say that they are false and fixed. In early recovery when sometimes, during active addiction, all you've heard is that you are useless, bad, weak-willed, dirty, or a failure, then it is difficult to shift those core beliefs. This shifting can start in Twelve-Step meetings with people learning they are ill and not bad. A common saying is, 'I'm an ill person trying to get well, not a bad person trying to be good'. Likewise, CBT recognises that these core beliefs are essential to the way we perceive our relationships with others, our relationship with ourselves, and, of course, with the world. Having these deep and negative self-judgements will be a major stumbling block to recovery and that underlying mentality of 'I'm not worth it' needs to be addressed.

Defence mechanisms

So, what are defence mechanisms and why are they applicable? A defence mechanism is a mental process initiated unconsciously to avoid experiencing conflict or anxiety and to protect oneself from shame, anxiety, loss of self-esteem, or other unacceptable feelings or thoughts. Drugs and alcohol may have been the initial coping strategy to deal with shame, anxiety, loss of self-esteem, or other unacceptable feelings or thoughts, but somewhere along the line, the avoidance of these feelings becomes a very strong and inbuilt defence mechanism. They can be considered as forms of insanity when put into Twelve-Step language.

When as teenagers, people discovered that alcohol gave them confidence, allowed them to socialise, and helped them forget their awful living conditions, then the cycle started. Using drugs or alcohol as a coping strategy leads to the development of further problems, and another layer of psychological defences will manifest in order to protect oneself from the consequences of the drug and alcohol use. Some of these are as follows:

Denial

Denial is a defence mechanism in which a person unconsciously rejects thoughts, feelings, needs, wishes, or external realities that they would not be able to deal with if they got into the conscious mind. One of the symptoms of addiction is denial. If a person refuses to believe that substance abuse is a problem for them they will be very unlikely to change their behavior. Even if the destruction caused by the addiction is obvious to everyone else, the addict may not see it. The person may have a host of explanations for why their life is in such a mess but denial means that they are unable to consider the real reasons.

Projection

The person using projection focuses on the fault in another person, and disproportionately criticises or focuses on it as an alternative to admitting and coping with it in themselves. An example of this for someone with an alcohol problem may be: 'I drink because my wife fights so much with me that I get sad, depressed, and angry with her.' In this case, it will often be the other way around. The fights with the wife are because of the drinking and the addict has projected the blame onto the other person.

Repression

Notedly, the first defence mechanism discovered by Freud, and some say the most important, is repression. This is where painful or traumatic memories are deliberately forgotten or pushed out of consciousness. It helps someone avoid feelings of guilt, shame, and anxiety. In the long term, it is considered an unsuccessful defence since it involves pushing the painful memories into the unconscious where they will cause anxiety.

Consider that someone with an alcohol problem wakes up in the morning with little recall of what happened the night before, is scared to face his family, and can tell by the reaction of his wife that last night was difficult, to say the least (a story I often hear). Instead of sitting down to discuss the issues and cover what went wrong, the alcoholic will (sometimes, not always) pretend that last night was a one-off, that it is the last time it will happen, and everything is good. The family members may also buy into this lie and everyone will pretend to be jolly and all is right with the world. The drunk overcompensates perhaps with flowers, etc., and the events from the night before are pushed to the back of the mind. They are not really gone but aren't talked about. Later in the day, the alcoholic has a creeping feeling of guilt and sadness and has no tangible answer that he is willing to accept. He picks up another drink.

Displacement

Simply speaking, this is taking something out on the wrong person! Here the individual becomes emotionally affected by person A and then takes it out on person B. For example, the stressed worker coming home and abusing their partner. I sometimes hear this from people in recovery who talk about their attitudes and aggression towards others when drinking, even though the other person was blameless. There is also another side to displacement that if we consider the word in a broader context applies to people, particularly in early recovery. If we consider that the drinking has become a routine pattern of daily living then how does one replace that and make a change. In early recovery, the addict may resort to overworking, or obsessively talking about their drug of choice. They may resort to overeating, be obsessed with relationships and sex, or they may need to go to fellowship meetings every day (or even more). Many of these things, in early recovery, are absolutely necessary to avoid taking that first drink or drug. It does, however, become a problem if some of the replacement activities are counterproductive or if they continue for too long.

Humour

Humour helps some of us cope with stressful situations. When people experience stressful situations they sometimes cover up the stress or pain involved by looking for, or creating, humour around the situation. Instead of discussing the disasters of the office party the night before the drinker will concentrate on the funny parts of the evening and avoid, or repress, the parts of the evening that were uncomfortable or downright embarrassing.

Reaction formation

Here the person has a strong reaction against his own inner desires: e.g., 'I hate drug users.' Recently, on visiting a UK prison, I heard talk of a guy with a reaction formation against people with alcohol problems. Although his offences were always committed when drunk, and his last offence got him imprisoned, he did not want to go onto the recovery wing because he did not want to be with the drunks.

Rationalisation

Here the person uses warped logic, often very convincingly, to attribute cause or explanation. If a person is faced with giving up their drug of choice they may rationalise that it would mean living a life of misery. They create a belief that they would never be able to enjoy themselves again and it would be more like serving a prison sentence than living.

Introjection

An unconscious process by which a person incorporates into his or her own psychic apparatus the characteristics of another person or object. Introjection occurs when we take on the attitudes of others, usually influential or authoritative persons. This may include emotions, behaviors, and perceptions. I find this an interesting idea. The fact is that if you grow up in a drug-taking culture, or experience peer pressure, you are likely to take drugs, and the same with alcohol (of course, there are those who reject drugs and alcohol totally because of that environment). This also confirms for me why people need to have recovery communities and fellowships like AA. If people are mixing with others in a culture of sobriety, then they will pick up those attitudes and beliefs as part of a psychological process. It then follows that if they return to a drinking or using environment they will have little chance of survival.

Step Two conclusion

Both models recognise the need for change. The Twelve Steps have an emphasis on higher powers and sanity, which is in line with the CBT concept of changing a belief system to help personal growth. Both models require the gathering of evidence and both believe that there are plenty of areas of thinking that need to be worked on and improved in order to combat addiction.

Chapter Three

Step Three

'Made a decision to turn our will and our lives over to the care of God as we understood Him.'

This book is not about converting anybody to God. I have no intention of trying to turn anyone into a believer. My focus in this book is to try and understand what is going on for people who find recovery using the Twelve-Step method. Step Eleven will focus more on God and why there may be some tremendous benefits of not fighting this word or concept.

Refocusing

In early recovery, the mental obsession with drugs or alcohol, as mentioned in Step One, is incredible. Anyone in early recovery has the challenge of moving away from the obsessional thinking that can dominate their every waking moment. They need the ability to be able to refocus their thoughts onto the kind of positive thinking that will move them into long-term recovery. Anyone who has found recovery knows how difficult it is to stop their head thinking about things.

In Step Three, making a decision helps with the focusing issue. When a person finds their mind wondering back to old obsessional thinking or thoughts, considered negative, a person can remind themselves that they have 'made a decision' to change. This gives them permission to stop and refocus. The idea is to start off gently, take a gentle walk and concentrate on the sights and sounds, see the flowers or trees, notice people smiling, make eye contact. If stuck in traffic, when those feelings of irritation creep in, take a breath and pause, thank your lucky stars, higher power, rehab, or counsellor and look around (if safe to do so) and notice the colours of other cars, look for something you may not have noticed before, see the names of shops, relax. When reflecting on these refocusing moments congratulate yourself on your success.

Motivation/willingness

The *Twelve Steps and Twelve Traditions* is the second main text used in AA and is promoted alongside the 'big book' it defines and identifies the Twelve Steps and Twelve traditions,

Step Three in the *Twelve and Twelve* identifies only one key, willingness. This is greatly tied in with motivation, which, in itself, leads to action. The fellowship of AA says the only requirement for fellowship is a desire to stop drinking. CBT, particularly the coaching style, focuses attention on finding out if a person truly wants to achieve change.

In my experience, this is a progressive state. (But isn't forced by AA.) People may initially be attending meetings for external reasons: they have been told to or they are mandated to. Some of these reasons could be:

- My husband/wife wants me to go.

- I must do this for the kids.

- My job is threatened if I don't attend.

- I have a court appearance so should go.

- My doctor says I must give up the booze.

There are many variations on these examples, and they are often characterised by the use of words like 'must' and 'should'. These indicate the person is being driven by an external motivation and has not considered going for them self. They have accepted it 'for the sake of others'.

The good news is that it can still work. There is the very real possibility that if a person continues to attend meetings and listens then they will, no doubt, find a connection, get motivated, and gain a willingness to change. They will see others are genuine and will be able to relate to the stories being told. They will find that they have met a group of people who speak the same language and share the same experiences. Somewhere along this path, most people will realise that they have to do recovery for themselves in order to make everything else work and the motivation becomes internal. A quote from *Alcoholics Anonymous* says, 'If we put our recovery first, then everything that comes second will be first class'. It sometimes takes a while to realise this and understand it.

It is impossible to completely feel and imagine what something will be like! This is partly because we change as people over time, and so the person who reaches the goal may not be the person who started in the first place. We then realise that the journey is the most important part, as *Alcoholics Anonymous* says, 'progress not perfection'.

Taking action can sometimes be difficult and procrastination is an easy trap to fall into. Have a look at the list below from *The Magic of Thinking Big* by David Schwartz.

Don't wait until conditions are perfect – If you're waiting to start until conditions are perfect, you probably never will. There will always be something that isn't quite right.

Be a doer – Practice doing things rather than thinking about them.

Do you want to start exercising? The longer an idea sits in your head without being acted on, the weaker it becomes. After a few days, the details get hazy. After a week it's forgotten completely.

Remember that ideas don't bring success – Ideas are important, but they're only valuable after they've been implemented. If you have an idea that you really believe in, do something about it. Unless you take action, it will never go anywhere.

Use action to cure fear – Have you ever noticed that the most difficult part of public speaking is waiting for your turn to speak? Action is the best cure for fear. The most difficult time to take action is the very first time. After the ball is rolling, you'll build confidence and things will keep getting easier. Kill fear by taking action and build on that confidence.

Start your creative engine mechanically – One of the biggest
misconceptions about creative work is that it can only

be done when inspiration strikes. If you wait for inspiration to slap you in the face, your work sessions will be few and far between. If you need to write something, (Step Four, inventory) force yourself to sit down and write. Put pen to paper. Explore or doodle. By moving your hands, you'll stimulate the flow of ideas and inspire yourself.

Live in the present – Focus on what you can do in the present moment. Don't worry about what you should have done last week or what you might be able to do tomorrow. The only time you can affect is the present. If you speculate too much about the past or the future you won't get anything done. Tomorrow or next week frequently turns into never.

Get down to business immediately – It's common practice for people to socialise and make small talk at the beginning of meetings. The same is true for individual workers. These distractions will cost you serious time if you don't bypass them and get down to business immediately.

Making decisions

While there are a wide variety of decision-making techniques and tools, many tend to revolve around the same key principles of figuring out the decision that needs to be made, considering and researching the options, and reviewing the decision once it's been made.

Making decisions is the leading part of Step Three and integral to CBT. CBT provides people with clear models on making and committing to decisions. Even when decisions are frightening, there is no clear decision to be made, or people have difficulty trusting and believing in their decisions, a cognitive approach can and will help. From the perspective of turning your will and life over to a higher power (which can be of ones own own choosing) and having faith in that decision, both the Twelve Steps and CBT demand belief and faith that the process will work.

The simplest decision-making tool that is universally recognised is the Pros and Cons list. For those of you that have not used one, it is simply two lists. One side has the positive aspects of the decision and the other has the negative.

I have a decision to make. Do I do it (**whatever** it is) or not?	
Pro	**Con**
I'll get support	People will know my secret
I can sort out my life problems	It won't be easy
I will have somewhere to live	I will have to follow house rules
My family will benefit	I will have to be open and honest with my family

When faced with a decision, use this simple tool to help in the process.

Stress

Introducing the topic of stress within Step Three may not fit everyone's idea of what this Step is about. From a CBT perspective, trying to make any decision while feeling overly stressed or pressured can lead to an unwise decision being made. On the other end of this spectrum, we find stress to be part of the catalyst for motivation and change. The Twelve Steps reminds people that everything should be in balance and the theory of CBT suggests the same. Too much stress and we cannot function; a person feels anxiety, can't sleep and is irritable, restless and discontent. Too little stress (or lack of drive) and a person's motivation may disappear, the reason to change becomes unimportant, and they may not be bothered to take action. Too little stress is often a trap that leads to relapse (see the Superman Effect). After a couple of months or so in recovery, stress is reduced and a person no longer feels motivated to continue to change. They have a feeling of contentment and mistake this for being the end of the journey. This highlights the importance of the maintenance Steps (Ten, Eleven, Twelve).

People need to learn a different perspective on stress, recognise the need for balance, and practice some tools that can help them manage their stress and make good decisions.

Some good measures to consider for a long recovery are:

- **Reduce stress.** Avoid conflict and triggers that are obvious, change social circles, remove that number from your phone, change jobs, leave a destructive relationship, and try some relaxation techniques.

- **Channel stress.** When practised, a person can feel stress or tension rising. Get them to channel it into something constructive. It is amazing what a once-hopeless alcoholic can achieve when they channel themselves properly.

- **Release stress.** If stress has built to become anger, or it is excessive, then find a way to relieve it. Go down the gym or play sport, relax and get emotional support, or find some way of venting it. There are some opposing views on using the gym or sport to release stress and the use of relaxation to calm it. Some say that the physical exertion can feed the stress and some say that burying it by forcing oneself to relax is storing it up for a big explosion. Find out what works best for the individual.

- **Stress resources.** When a person suspects that stress may be on the way, or they have a difficult event coming up, then a number of actions may increase a person's ability to cope. Certainly, from a Twelve-Step perspective, going to more meetings can be a lifesaver. Helping others or doing service, can take the focus off the stress. Don't try to cope with stress alone, talk to someone, pray more, eat healthier and try to find out what those individual resources are that apply to oneself. Fill up that toolbox.

- **Have a plan.** One of the repeated mantras of Twelve-Step recovery is 'a day at a time', which can be a great lifesaver. However, within that, there needs to be a running plan of where a person wants to end up. What are the reasons for getting into recovery, what does the person want to change long term? Is their job stressing them out? It may be necessary to survive the daily grind one day at a time with thinking along the lines of 'I can't win the war in a day but I can win the daily battles'. If someone feels they are stuck where they are forever, then it is easy to become depressed and lose motivation. Day-at-a-time thinking is a means to an end.

- **Laughter.** 'What is there to laugh about?' can be dominant thinking in early recovery. It is quite common for someone to think they are in the wrong room when they go to their first meeting because of the amount of laughter. Laughter is great for releasing stress. As a person's recovery progresses, they will find this easier to do. Sometimes they are amazed they can laugh without the world collapsing in on them. There are many genuine physiological reasons why laughter is beneficial.

Lifestyle

Making a decision in Step Three is about changing lifestyle. Someone trying to get sober will realise this, but that doesn't make it easy.

Work out what needs to be changed. Stopping the use of alcohol and drugs is just the tip of the iceberg. CBT would also say that some exploration needs to be done in relation to the lifestyle problems supporting the current dysfunctional situation. Not all of these are solvable and there may be conflicts with what needs to be done to achieve sobriety. For instance, the partner in a relationship that leaves them feeling trapped. It may be that for a person to thrive and enjoy their recovery, the toxic relationship has to end. This is not always possible for many reasons. Those people that say 'just leave him' may not realise how difficult this is.

Stopping drugs or alcohol leaves a big, big gap in a person's life. They need to find something healthy to do to fill that gap. Exercise helps in lots of ways and some people like this and some don't. Often people discover they have a 'brain' that is capable of learning and will engage in all sorts of education or start new hobbies or return to old ones they gave up due to their addiction.

Step Three conclusion

Whatever the circumstances, Step Three is the point at which a person decides to change many of the fundamental elements in their life that will not sustain a healthy recovery.

Making a decision is about committing to following the guidance of others. Many will see the 'God' word and shut down without having the capacity, patience, or vision to realise or understand this is not a religious thing. Exactly as in CBT, a person who is in crisis is very unlikely to think their way out of that situation on their own. It is important that they recognise the need for help. This Step is about self-development, recognising the need for that development, and reaching out for help and guidance as to how to better manage lifestyle, choices, and behaviors.

Chapter Four
Step Four

*'Made a searching and fearless moral
inventory of ourselves.'*

This chapter will consider what is meant by the 'wrongs'
mentioned in *Alcoholics Anonymous*, the importance of
looking at the past, recognising where fault lies, and
recognising feelings. Because of the reference to them in
Alcoholics Anonymous, this chapter will also look at the
'seven deadly sins' and consider them in little more depth.

Looking at the past

In CBT, the past is important as it will lead the therapist to
identify patterns of behavior and perceptions that will give
rise to the design of disrupting models and help study
behaviors in depth. This is also true for identifying deep-
rooted problems and behaviors that may be key to current
issues. It is important to remember the past always has a
part to play in current behavior. In Step Four, there are
some keywords of note: fear, resentment, and anger. These
are connected to sex relations, self-esteem, security,

personal relationships, and pride. Some of these we will cover later.

Past problems

It is an easy trap to fall into, thinking that your past will determine your future, and, of course, there is some truth to that. In recovery, this can be a major hurdle for some. Believing that they will fail because they have failed before (because of their wrongs) can be a difficult barrier to overcome. AA mentions not regretting the past and not wishing to shut the door on it. But how does a person do that? What mechanisms are at play? CBT takes a look at core beliefs – those that are negative and unhealthy – and suggests ways of tackling them. For instance, a person who believes they are bad needs to remember there are good things about them. People believing themselves to be failures can look at their strengths and achievements. When completing a daily inventory, as in Step Ten, remember that in the *Twelve and Twelve*, it reminds people that 'inventory taking is not always done in red ink'. We will have done some good things and some right things during the day. Sometimes people might need help to recognise that.

Replacing old beliefs with new is not done alone and people often need help. In Step Four and, of course, in CBT we are looking at a person's history in connection to how they function now, and although CBT does not dwell on the past like other therapies, it does consider the importance of the past in developing unhealthy attitudes and beliefs. Like Step Four's inventory taking, a person is looking for those repeated or powerful errors in thinking that dictate current behaviors. Identification is a significant part of change.

Fear

Fear is described in *Alcoholics Anonymous* as 'an evil and corroding thread' that touches people throughout their lives during active addiction. In CBT, fear is recognised as a valid enemy that can be triggered in stressful or difficult situations. In both models, you will hear or read FEAR often expressed as Face Everything and Recover. There is great mileage in this but caution needs to be remembered. Pushing or forcing a person too far into a fearful situation can be dangerous.

The exposure to the stressor or trigger needs to be challenging but not so much it causes a relapse. There are processes at work that mean if exposure to the fear is slow and safe, they can lead a person to build up an immunity to it. CBT also recognises the value in scaling. For example, 0 = no fear, 10 = very fearful. In this case, you can scale for a before and after measure. What was the anticipated level of fear 0-10 and what was the actual fear level 0-10? Often, a person scales the actual fear lower than the anticipated fear. Once a person measures where they are, using a scale, it gives a benchmark that they can then use to evidence progress. If someone is fearful of going to a meeting, get them to do this exercise so they can measure their own progress.

Resentment

The number one offender according to the 'big book'! Resentments can manifest in many ways and in AA terms, resentment is a flaw in a person's make up that causes failure and destroys more alcoholics than anything else. Resentments can hijack thoughts, cause sleepless nights, be the cause of grinding teeth into tiny stumps and be a great excuse for justifying all sorts of behaviors.

When someone has a resentment, they need to realise that the person they have a resentment about may not even know it. They are sleeping soundly while the person with the grudge is wide awake with the offender running around in their head. A way must be found to let it go. In the Twelve Steps, Steps Four and Five are there to help the beginning of this process of moving on.

The guilt that a person can attach to resentments can empower feelings of blame. A person occasionally actively searches for someone else to hold responsible for the disasters of the past (sometimes as a subconscious defence mechanism and sometimes deliberately) looking for the evidence that the other person was at fault. Harbouring a grudge only leads to hostility, distracting us from joy and peace, and resentments can become embedded bitter themes that dictate our lives. Step Four helps people work out who owns what part in things and who was responsible for those different parts.

It is not uncommon for adults to blame themselves for things that happened as children. Holding on to thoughts like 'Daddy left home because of me' or 'It's my fault he assaulted me. If I hadn't dressed in that way he would have left me alone' can be common. The resentment towards self sometimes has no consideration that the situation was unfair. The young self had no part to play in it that can be blamed or apportioned guilt to. This can be a powerful thing for a person to find out about themselves. They have been holding on to guilt and blame for something they needn't have. Of course, the desire to escape from guilt, whether conscious or not, really feeds into the need to pick up a drink or drug again.

Anger

In the 'big book' anger is described with what I think are wonderfully crafted words, 'the dubious luxury of normal men', and the point is made that if people are to live (in recovery) then they have to be free of anger. It is an incredibly powerful gateway back to active addiction. When angry, people become irrational and compulsive, and they are more likely to pick up a drink.

Anger can certainly be bad for relationships, a person's health, or the way people regard themselves. Ways of anger showing itself physically include clenched teeth or fists, trembling or shaking, flushed skin, feeling hot and sweaty, and, of course, if continued long term can lead to levels of stress that become hazardous to health. Having a raised heart rate because of anger will no doubt take its toll in the long term.

Are people quick to anger and is there an obvious shortcoming/thinking error at play? Having a low frustration level can be part of the problem, particularly if a person feels that another is getting in the way of their all-important goal. At that point, using language like 'I can't stand it' won't help. Having high expectations of others and little tolerance for others' failings can be the cause of many a grouchy feeling. In Step Four, it reminds people to show others 'the same tolerance, pity, and patience that we would show a sick friend'. CBT reminds us to do the same thing and accept people as fallible human beings. It reminds us not to use negative words such as 'useless' or 'bad' not only because these are gross over generalisations but, by putting people down, we will reduce our overall respect for them in all matters. We need to remember that just because a person behaves in a certain way in a given situation doesn't mean they will act like that in all situations. Repeatedly telling people they are bad can lead to that person believing they are bad in every aspect of their being. They, therefore, act badly whenever they can, after all, they have got a reputation to keep up. We need love and tolerance of others, but what of ourselves?

People may default to anger for a number of reasons. It can feel better to attack than be attacked. For instance, if I listen to people and they make comments about me then I may be reminded of how low I feel about myself; best to treat them with hostility and put them down rather than let them have the opportunity to put me down. As a person develops in their recovery and their self-worth develops, then the defensive anger will diminish.

CBT also highlights that there are healthy angers and unhealthy angers. Healthy anger can be of use in certain circumstances, for instance when anger spurs a person on to assert their rights, or you're trying to push that last set of reps at the gym. The difference is one of intensity and experiencing no loss of control on an emotional level. One of the great issues for people in recovery is the use of self-will. (Being powerless does not mean you have no self-will). Applying self-will in the right way takes a bit of learning. If it is spurred on by a rage that has got out of control, then it is a very dangerous thing indeed. If it is intense but controlled then it can push people to do great things.

I'm using a bit of anger now to spur me on to write this book, but I must remind myself of those wonderful words at the beginning of this section and that the use of anger can be a dubious area not to be relied upon.

Self-esteem

Often, people in early recovery can be convinced it will all go wrong and they will fail. This can come from a place of low self-opinion, which is connected with feelings of shame, guilt and anxiety - a self-esteem issue that can be a crippling handicap. Feeling like you're a failure in life, especially when people treat you as such, can be an underpinning issue that has a person believing that they will not achieve when trying to find recovery; 'Why should

I? I've failed at everything else.' This may be the result of good experiences in the past that have gone wrong. A person has learned to fear those feelings of positiveness because when things are good they will inevitably go bad. Many a person has said to me that they feel great now they are in recovery but know it won't last long and are waiting for the crash. This does not have to be true and can sometimes be a form of sabotaging oneself with a self-fulfilling prophecy.

Trauma may be a reason for low self-esteem. Occasionally, a person will have a traumatic experience where they thought all was going well and they felt good about themselves. Then something very negative happened. In these situations, the person can become afraid of expecting to feel positive and are afraid of having a healthy self-image, in case 'it happens again'. Helping a person to see that this is a form of overgeneralisation that can be overcome is a way forward.

Sometimes, people who are unfamiliar with the Twelve Steps can see this step as a very self-blaming exercise. They say that 'Finding out and examining your moral inventory is surely one way to reinforce the negatives that have happened'. We need to remember that, as with CBT, if a person does not know what's gone wrong in the past then they will never know how they can change it in the future. So, Step Four becomes a building block to move on from these past mistakes, to examine the real facts, and to recognise the power that the past has had over a person's current beliefs and actions.

In my experience, most people find out that their frightening and awful deep and dark secrets weren't that bad after all!

Scapegoats

A trap that people can fall into is 'scapegoating' and this connects with why the 'willingness' in this Step is an important part of moving on. Sometimes, the blame for things gone wrong is laid at the wrong feet and people may need to make amends for blaming others for the things that have gone wrong in their own life, of course this ties in directly with Step Eight but I have chosen to (partly) focus on it here. People have to understand that they may have seen things upside down and laid blame unfairly. An example is a husband who blames his drinking on his wife because she left him. In reality, she left him because of the drinking.

People's anger and resentments towards others may be cruel, illogical, or twisted out of shape. There may be some comfort in denying responsibility for things or even some gratification in blaming others. Events may be skewed or misrepresented laying the blame on others or anyone but them self.

In the 'big book', it mentions listing people, institutions, or principles touching on the theme of globalising blame. In CBT, it mentions that some people can fall into blame towards many things, thus removing responsibility from them self. This globalisation of blame can include things like 'God', it could be that they see themselves as having bad DNA or a medical issue, or that their environment is wrong: 'it's this house', it's the fault of nature or society, or it's the fault of the police: 'I would not have ended up in jail if it wasn't for them'. The list goes on.

It is important to be able to work out whether someone might be avoiding responsibility, is in denial, has mental health issues that mean they genuinely have no understanding of their part in things, or whether they are just not willing to change. A good therapist or sponsor will have to respond to all of these things on an individual basis and take action accordingly.

In order to turn this around, a person needs to find the truth behind who or what is to blame. This may be done with a mapping exercise so as to drill down to each person in the situation and deal with each individually. It will also be of help for a person to acknowledge that they always have a part to play in things and they need to take responsibility for those things. By working on 'what's my part in it?' they can move from the place where 'it's not my fault, I was a victim' to becoming aware that 'victim thinking' can be an excuse to continue to hurt others. Again, this is a process that I often see recovering addicts move through. People go from the inner culture of blame to taking responsibility for change This is quite empowering and often precedes lots of internal movement forward.

Naming feelings

It's not uncommon for people in early recovery to have difficulty defining or feeling feelings. The old sayings that the 'good thing about recovery is you get your feelings back and the bad thing about recovery is you get your feelings back' is only partly true. For starters, people don't know how to feel, what it is their feeling, and have difficulty defining one feeling from another.

There are many feelings some of which are listed over the next few pages, for anyone in early recovery feelings and emotions are a new minefield that is difficult to walk let alone have control over. It is OK not to understand feelings. Often people don't know what they are or how they feel; this takes time and work.

Generally, it is considered there are eight basic emotions that all others stem from, these are:

- Fear – feeling afraid

- Anger – feeling angry

- Sadness – feeling sad

- Joy – feeling happy

- Disgust – feeling something unpleasant

- Surprise – being unprepared for something

- Trust – a positive emotion of having faith in something

- Anticipation – looking forward positively to something that is going to happen

It seems easy to write but acting in a way that is opposite to your feelings can be a good way of counteracting them. The founders of CBT say that if you can turn a negative strategy on its head then you are on the way to finding a solution. For example:

Avoiding situations that make a person anxious or frightened only leaves a person still fearful of that situation. Using drugs and alcohol to cope with fearful situation leads a person to believe that they can only cope with that situation if they have a drink or drug inside of them. I am often staggered at the number of celebrities who have been given drugs to cope with stage fright. This slippery slope rarely has a good outcome. The feelings generated, which a person drinks or uses drugs for, are still there. The next time those feelings make an appearance (or whatever it is that makes a person drink or drug) the feelings are only masked by the drug of choice, they don't go away they are only hidden. Heres the catch, not only has a person not dealt with the feelings, whether it be fear, anxiety or something else, but as the body's tolerance to whatever it is they take increases then more of the drug is often needed to cope with the situation. A person stands the chance of building a dependency that is sure to spill over into other aspects of their lives.

Feelings about feelings

It is quite common to have feelings about feelings, which is something CBT refers to as meta-emotions. They are mentioned quite often in the 'big book' and the 'Twelve and Twelve'. For example, 'self-righteous anger' is when a person feels good about their anger; they feel as if they have a right to feel it and positively look forward to taking out on the person who deserves their wrath. Afterwards, they feel guilty about their actions.

One of the problems with meta-emotions, especially in addiction, is that they may prevent people from dealing with the primary cause of their situation. Instead of seeing the underlying depression that they have, they concentrate on the feelings of guilt from last night's fiasco or focus on the actions they took instead of trying to find the underlying problem. As with denial, the person unintentionally misdirects their thinking away from the real problem and looks at other minor issues as the real cause. In recovery meetings, people often talk about the cycle of guilt they go through when waking. They are unsure of what happened last night, who they offended, or who they hurt. These guilty feelings seem to be the important ones and take priority in a person's thinking. Later in the day, they seem to be so overwhelming that 'a little drink' seems to be the right thing to do so as to 'just take the edge off' and so they get drunk all over again and wake up the next day with the guilt again. They have unintentionally missed the point. As with the ASAM definition of addiction, the primary cause of all this guilt is the addiction itself. Without the addiction, a person wouldn't be hurting their family, wouldn't be embarrassing themselves at the work party, or wouldn't have been in trouble with the authorities.

CBT is basically saying that a person may have fixed ideas about which emotions they find acceptable or not acceptable. It's not uncommon among people with drug or alcohol problems for them to believe that they are weak and lack willpower, they will have been told so many times. If a person has grown up in a culture that spouts phrases like 'real men don't cry' or 'don't cry over spilt milk' (and many of us have) then people may not have been allowed to express feelings. They will feel bad about feeling bad. The internal conflict of wanting to scream or cry, when not allowed, creates a guilt cycle which people then use or drink on.

Control

Needing to be in control of emotions and feelings can leave a person having more worry about their inability to control the impossible. A good piece of therapeutic advice is to stop the fight. A piece of guidance often recommended in Twelve-Step recovery is to 'let yourself feel those feelings', sit with them, don't run away and let them work themselves through.

When? How? Who? Whom else? Why?

Similar to the grudge list that is created in Step Four, many therapies use a method that, at its core, is the same idea. These therapies consider the above questions to being a key to understanding and changing perceptions and behaviors. The similarities are real so let's have a look at the questions in more depth. They may not always come out in the order of 'When? How? Who? Whom else? Why?', so if a person is feeling anxious (affects me) but is not sure why or where it comes from it may take a while to drill down to the cause of the anxiety and find out the 'why' of it.

When?

It is important to find out the 'when' of things, to find out when the problem shows itself, or rears its ugly head. There may be connections to places or environments that best be avoided in the future or that can be worked through to lower its impact or hold over the person. Finding out when resentments were picked up is a key to letting them go.

In some people, the 'when' may be very specific and, in recovery, can be important in identifying triggers. The practical approach in AA means you may often hear people say things like 'Well, walk a different way then,' in response to the sponsee who eludes to always feeling huge waves of anxiety when they walk past the local wine bar. Of course, this Step is closely tied to Step Eight and we will retouch on this area in that Step.

How?

How is it impacting on the person? Do they feel low confidence, anxiety, are there any physical signs? I.e. sweating, blushing, or stammer, etc. As in the 'big book', how does it affect a person's self-esteem, fear, security, relations, or pride?

Who?

The 'who' refers to the client themselves. It means, who were they being at the time the problem occurred? In CBT, this is important as the role a person is in at the time of the incident can influence the outcome and feelings around the situation. For instance, a parent who is very confident with their children may be very timid and frightened in the workplace. If we understand the context of the situation then we are more able to find a solution. This may be important when creating a Step Four inventory, there is a difference that needs to be examined. If someone was drunk when they lashed out at another – or if they were sober – what is the difference? This needs to be examined.

Of course, they may also be resentful towards themselves and need to make note of this.

Whom else?

Refers to the others involved in the situation. This is the 'people, places, and things' that is often spoken about in Twelve-Step meetings. This phrase comes from one of the personal stories in the 'big book' called 'Acceptance Was the Answer'. This great teaching story helps people understand that the problem is within. When a person is disturbed (anxious, fearful, or angry, etc.) it is because the event that is occurring is unacceptable to the person experiencing it. People often blame others for their thoughts and feelings but the reality is that it is an inside job. When teaching I sometimes throw out the question 'Who in this group makes me angry?' After some feet shuffling and gazing at the floor from the participants, I inform them that 'I do'. It is the way I react to them or their behaviors that make me angry. We are so used to externalising our feelings and shifting the blame to others that when asked the above question, in a teaching situation, people immediately start to take the blame – guilty or not. When asking a similar question in this situation, 'Who in this group makes me happy?' You will observe members of your group trying to catch your eye so that you can point them out as the one. This is not a criticism of the people in the group but an observation that you can easily create. Of course, they look a little angry when you tell them the answer is, 'I do. I make me happy.'

Why?

This is the question that is about searching for the answers or causes of the problems. As mentioned above, it is about drilling down to the root causes, or the supposed root causes.

The Seven deadly sins

In the *Twelve and Twelve*, the Seven Deadly Sins are mentioned in Step Four and no self-respecting work would be complete without having a further look at those.

Envy

The desire to have an item, person, experience, or position that someone else possesses. This can lead to a harsh state of anger and hatred, which is obviously not healthy for recovery. Wishing you had someone else's things can give rise to gossip, negative comments, or downright hostility, all of which are dangerous emotions to engage in when in recovery. There is some fixed and rigid thinking connected with envy that may lead a person to obtain the desired item or state despite the consequences.

Gluttony

Excessive ongoing consumption of food or drink. Obvious connections here to addiction leading to overindulgence and overconsumption of food, drink, or other things to the point of extravagance, waste, and self-harm. Swapping one addiction for another is often mentioned in recovery and caution needs to be adhered to so that a person does not stop the booze and then finds them self compulsively eating.

Greed or avarice

An excessive pursuit of material possessions. When greed becomes a motivation, there is a danger of disregarding others' well-being which can lead to the exploitation of people. Greed can lead to people becoming fixated on what they want and finds them always trying to get hold of the one thing that will finally solve their problems. There are connections to people having an underlying sense of something lacking or unavailable, (sometimes addiction is described as a disease of 'more') an area commonly spoken about in recovery.

Lust

An uncontrollable passion or longing, especially for sexual desires. In early recovery, with a person's feelings and hormonal functions returning with a vengeance, lust can be a difficult area. There are many articles written about sex addiction in recovery with many links being made. Some descriptions of lust connect the word to overwhelming desires and cravings.

Pride

Excessive view of one's self without regard to others. In active addiction, pride can be a difficult conundrum connected with denial. In fellowship meetings, it is not uncommon to hear the phrase 'I was in the gutter looking down on people' meaning that a person still felt superior to others even though they were in a very low place.

Sloth

Excessive laziness or the failure to act and utilise one's talents. The Twelve Steps are a programme of action. You have to get up and do something and an attitude of laziness will do a person no good. During active addiction, there is a connection with people never completing things, staying at home all day, or not engaging with many sorts of activities including work or housework. Of course, there are other issues at play but the connection with laziness and a lack of motivation is too obvious to dismiss.

Wrath

Uncontrollable feelings of anger and hate towards another person. Resentment is the number one offender according to the 'big book' and this is very much connected to the state of wrath. It can become a dangerous 'all or nothing' scenario when a person loses control of their logical thinking and goes into a mode of destruction. Anger is the foe of many in recovery, leading to knee-jerk reactions and decisions that have not been thought through correctly.

Step Four conclusion

Discovering the underlying causes of a person's current problematic feelings and behaviors is the essence of Step Four's 'moral inventory' and, of course, this is the same in CBT. The 'When? How? Who? Whom else? Why?' method that CBT uses is about finding out those unhealthy thoughts and could easily be CBT's equivalent of a 'moral inventory'. The focus within this chapter has included a more defined look at some of those specific issues and finer details that become people's handicaps. Both methods are aligned when it comes to getting to root causes and then using tools to change or address them.

Chapter Five

Step Five

'Admitted to God, to ourselves and to another human being the exact nature of our wrongs.'

So, what are the exact nature of our wrongs? Again, CBT says that if we don't know what these things are we can't change them. So self-awareness is a key to getting well. In this section, among other things, we will be examining errors in thinking, the significance of telling others, and the importance of whom we tell.

Confession?

Step Five is about telling your story and the importance of this. Again, CBT and the Twelve Steps have recognised an important idea. Talking to other people is important. Talking to someone you respect and trust is doubly important. Many of the studies and important theories that focus on talking therapies come back to a similar message; the most important part of any therapeutic relationship is the connection between client and counsellor or sponsor and sponsee. As mentioned in the introduction, Carl

Rogers' number one criterion for successful therapy is the Therapist-Client Psychological Contact. This first condition simply states that a relationship between therapist and client must exist in order for the client to achieve positive personal change. So, talking to another person about personal stuff when you trust them is a good idea and, on its own, aids the healing process. I'm categorically **not** saying sponsees are clients.

Secondly, talking to another person works for everyone; young or old, rich or poor, professional or long-term unemployed. It doesn't matter, as long as trust and respect are there. There is lots of evidence to show that talking to others can resolve physical symptoms and release feelings that have been 'swallowed down'. Talking helps shape things, so, rather than a vague and painful problem sitting in your head that you can't put your finger on, talking helps define it and makes it easier to recognise for what it is. Talking about a problem can make the problem clearer.

Addiction can be an illness of isolation, so a person sitting there with all this stuff in their head is going to find it very difficult to move on from that stuff unless they break that isolation. Talking to another starts that process (by isolation, I don't just mean living like a hermit; people with addiction can be in a room with a thousand people and still feel lonely and isolated). Knowing that you are not alone and that others share similar experiences, stories, ideas and crazy thinking goes a long way in helping a person move away from the bonds of isolation. Besides, talking helps rewire a person's brain to work in a different and new way. A bit like medication but hopefully with fewer side effects, talking can help lift a low mood by having a direct effect on the depressed parts of the brain. Remember, sayings like 'A problem shared is a problem halved' don't just come from nowhere.

God, ourselves and another human being?

Why the three? Why doesn't Step Five just say to 'God', or just 'ourselves', or just someone else? A very good question and one that I think needs answering. In the 'big book', it quite rightly identifies that at the end of someone's drinking they will not be able to identify the 'true from the false'. This is not just because they are drunk, it is because their brain processing capabilities have been greatly diminished. There are all sorts going on, apart from PAWS, which is a whole other topic.

When your mental health is in a state of poor functionality it can be easy to delude yourself. God may well be listening, but I truly have no idea as to whether he, she, or it is. However, in a poor state of mental health, I can easily convince myself that God is listening, has replied, and given the OK for my appalling actions and behavior. He may even give me permission directly to steal a car or run naked down the street. Yes, I'm sure that you can agree, relying on self for correct and reliable answers, when in a state of ill mental health can be a hazardous exercise at best. So, we need another human being to bring balance, other points of view and possibly truths that the sponsee cannot see. Even if a person's mental health is not that damaged, the need for input from others is clearly a good idea, if only to shine a new light on a past situation that the sponsee has not seen before.

Finally, why to self? It's obvious and a cornerstone of many therapies that if a person cannot see the problem, then they cannot address it. As my brother likes to say to me, 'blind people are blind'.

Cognitive distortions

These errors are common to lots of strands of psychology and counselling. Sometimes referred to as 'errors in thinking or mind traps' you will find many examples of them, and these may indeed be the exact nature of some people's wrongs if we put them into the Twelve-Step context. For this book, and this Step, we will be covering the headings as below. There may be more that you can find if you search. Helping a person understand and recognise that they may have developed unhelpful, inaccurate and negative thoughts and emotions that however sound, rational and true to them are just not true is a vital part of this Step. If people can start to see some of their own connections with the thinking errors below, then they will be moving forward with challenging the feelings that keep them locked in a dark place.

Personalising

Unlike a person who is narcissistic (believing that all good things stem from them), such people blame all disasters on themselves. If it goes wrong, it must be their fault. Within Step Five, the emphasis is on finding out what is true and what isn't. A sponsee who automatically concludes that all the wrongs of the past were their fault, even when there is no evidence to support this, may be personalising, that is to say, that they are assuming responsibility when there are no grounds for doing so. An example of this manifesting itself in recovery could be, 'I won't speak at Twelve-Step meetings or in groups because everyone will judge me and think that what I say is awful.'

Catastrophising

Often referred to as 'turning molehills into mountains'. When looking at the past and creating an inventory, can the sponsee see any times that they have blown things out of proportion? Are some of the situations that they have identified fairly neutral but have been given over-exaggerated importance? The role of the counsellor or sponsor is to identify these areas and bring them into balance. People's addiction stories often recount odd episodes of catastrophising. For instance, picking up a drink or drug when a light bulb blew. This small incident was so overwhelmingly massive that they drank again.

Fortune telling

Here the person believes that they know what the outcome will be. Their crystal ball is active all the time and they are convinced that they know the outcome of many situations, which, of course, will be terrible. Looking at the past and trying to identify this as a cognitive distortion, the sponsee may be able to identify times when they predicted outcomes incorrectly or even affected outcomes because of their own negative predictions.

In early recovery, it can be common for a person to surmise all sorts of things if their sponsor, or a friend, fails to answer a phone call immediately. They may have a small resentment and feel a bit angry, possibly thinking, 'He's ignoring me because I'm not important' (mind reading); 'If I try to ring him again he will really think I am a loser and will certainly dump me' (fortune telling). A couple of hours later the sponsor returns the call apologising that he couldn't answer earlier as he was in caught up in another situation. A lot of angst that was self-imposed.

Mind reading

Similar to fortune telling, here the person believes they know what the other person is thinking about them. Again 'mind reading' mostly falls into the negative frame of thinking, with people believing that the thoughts others have about them are always awful. When examining the past, can a sponsee see any examples of this? Did this way of thinking ever drive them to make rash decisions the resulted in an item being present in their Step Four list? Are there resentments on that list that are based on assumptions rather than fact? When manifesting in current situations, does a sponsee say things like 'I went to a meeting and I know everyone there didn't like me'? This thinking is based on speculation and not evidence.

Emotional reasoning

Feelings are not facts. 'I feel therefore I am' is an assumption that can be regarded as a thinking error. Ever felt guilty when a police car is behind you, even though you have never committed a driving offence in your life? People with this error will believe the guilt, or fear, or shame and convince themselves it must be so. 'I am guilty because I feel guilty.' Many people will relate to this in their active addiction; feelings of guilt and shame even if their behavior was impeccable. It can soon develop into a circular process; drinking because of guilt and feeling guilty because of drink. During this step, it may be a good time to look for past episodes where the sponsee has judged them self as worthless when not true, because of feelings of failure.

With Post-Acute Withdrawal Syndrome, the body and mind are going through some major changes, hormones and chemicals that may have been depressed are starting to come alive again. This often leads a person to have all sorts of emotions and they often need support and reassurance that it is a process they are going through and the feelings have no real bases that need to be acted upon.

Overgeneralisation

Here, people make sweeping conclusions about people, things, environments, situations and ourselves, based on minor evidence that, again, is usually negative. For example, an interview goes badly, therefore, 'I am awful at all interviews'. Concluding that things will always go wrong because of that one time can be an error that leads to isolation and misery. In the context of Step Five, can the sponsee identify elements in them self that were forms of overgeneralisation? One I can think of is that often alcoholics think that everyone drinks like them when they are actively drinking, and 'What do you mean you don't have a drink at the end of the workday?' In recovery, people can often go to one meeting, not like it and judge all meetings to be the same.

Labelling

This is about judgement! People are 'good' or 'bad', yourself included. No one is allowed to be in the 'grey' zone of a mixture of both. Labelling is similar to black-and-white thinking but instead is more about a person's character. When people start to label themselves negatively, it can become self-defeating and within this step, it would be good for people to examine whether they have done that to themselves or not. Has your sponsee labelled them self as a loser because of the one time they screwed up? Did they then carry on with drinking or drugging because 'that's who I am'? Strangely enough, if we flip this on its head, labels can be helpful. I know many people outside of Twelve-Steps fellowships disagree with this but, for many, the identification with the label 'alcoholic' or 'addict' has helped many people to recovery. Me included.

In recovery, people need to be aware of the ability to falsely label people. Rather than more objectively thinking about the behavior of a person, they apply a label or two to the whole person. For example, instead of trying to understand why a certain person is late for meetings, they say, 'She is frequently late to meetings so, she must be irresponsible,' or 'Maybe she's not working her programme'. There is little consideration for what else may be going on.

Inflexibility

Here, the person is convinced that things 'should be that way'. They are unable to accept that things do not always go according to plan or that there is more than one set of rules in this world that might be different for other people. As an underlying issue and within the concept of this step, can the sponsee see times when they developed a grudge because others didn't do it the way it 'should be done'?

A minor example of this, which can have major consequences, is that of a person attending a meeting who sits in the same chair every week. One week they go and the chair is occupied by someone else, they get upset and never return to that meeting again and/or are resentful for several days or weeks.

Closed mind

Here, the person becomes closed-minded to any evidence to the contrary of their negative belief. So, even though the person can see something working for someone else, they believe it definitely won't work for them. I often see people trying to tackle their substance misuse with this false belief.

As part of this step, can a sponsee see times that they stubbornly refused to admit that others may be right? Can people connect it with their denial and give examples of being told by others that they were in trouble with drink or drugs but point blank refused to believe it? What examples can they find of this type of thinking that may have fuelled aspects of their Step Four inventory?

Disqualifying the positive /filtering

The person experiences something that at first sight is obviously positive. In order to disqualify it and remain closed-minded, however, they attach it to something else that is negative. Particularly when depressed, people don't only just ignore the positive but can quickly turn them into a negative by adding all sorts of false conclusions. This can be very destructive in a person's life. I've often heard people talk of all of the negative stuff that happened during their active addiction – 'nothing good ever happened' – only to find that in recovery they can now recall lots of great events throughout their lives. Their childhood was not all doom and gloom, they just saw it that way.

I recall a story someone once told. This person had a burning resentment towards her mother (whom she hadn't seen for fifteen years) because as a child she was never allowed to wear socks. Her mother never bought them for her, she was a cruel and wicked parent. When this person had been in recovery for a while she contacted her mother and re-established the relationship. It got better and better. One day at a family gathering her mother got out the family photo album, there were plenty of pictures of our now recovering person as a little girl. And guess what, she had socks on in every one of the pictures.

With regards to this error, in current situations around the Twelve Steps, an example that I often encounter can be observed sometimes when a newcomer goes to a meeting. They are made to feel welcome, people are friendly and offer telephone numbers or the chance to meet up for a coffee. The person that is new at the meetings dismisses the warm welcome surmising that 'they must be after something' and so the welcome was not genuine as there is an ulterior motive for it.

Low frustration tolerance

Catastrophising one's own frustrations and making unreasonable demands on self and others can lead to this cognitive distortion. This is also closely related to low discomfort tolerance, which is when a person can't stand the discomfort of negative emotions. These two issues can be major drivers in the alcoholic's perceived inability to cope with the world and everyone in it. This unintentional state of mind may be a trigger factor in many people's overwhelming feelings of discomfort that lead them to pick up another drink.

People with low frustration tolerance believe things like:

- The world owes them.

- Things should be the way they want them and if not, they can't tolerate them.

- Frustration is abhorrent and so must be avoided.

- Others should not be doing things that frustrate them either.

These remind me of page sixty in the 'big book', which covers the topic of the actor who 'wants to run the whole show' and is always trying to control everything. If all doesn't go according to his plan then his low frustration tolerance becomes worse and he decides to exert himself even more. As a person's recovery evolves, you see this type of thinking start to drop off and people start to appreciate the diversity of the world, other people, and especially meetings.

Step Five conclusion

Disclosing problematic thoughts, feelings, and behaviors to trusted others is a well-known solution to the secrecy and isolation of troublesome thinking. Step Five often leads a person to feel relief and freedom from the weight of all the baggage that has been clinging to them for years and keeping them in the cycle of addiction. Understanding which cognitive distortions may be trapping a person in their old thinking and behavior can be a pivotal point in ensuring that they are able to let go of their 'stuff'. This, of course, will be of great help in moving forward.

Chapter Six

Step Six

'Were entirely ready to have God remove all these defects of character.'

Focusing on character defects, this chapter will look at some of those recognised areas that are common to many and hinder a person's recovery. There are perhaps many more and some you may consider apply and some don't.

'Out of balance' is a term you may or may not like but from a Twelve-Step perspective, life is all about balance. People may have all of the defects mentioned below to some degree or other and that is how it should be. The problem, from this perspective, is when they get out of balance.

Of course, Step Six initially refers to the things a person has discovered about themselves in Step Five, but this is only the beginning. The importance of this Step being expanded on in the *Twelve and Twelve* becomes obvious.

The understanding that we need, to build character and work on patient improvement, becomes obvious as does the recognition that we will learn about character defects we didn't know about, that we will not wish to let go of some of them – may even enjoy a few – and even have some that we stubbornly refuse to give up. People can also disguise shortcomings as other things, using nice words to wrap them in so that they don't look so harsh. An example given in the 'big book' is that of dressing gluttony up as 'taking our comfort'.

Step Six says we will have to take a 'brand new venture into open-mindedness'. So, with an open mind have a look at the tool below. The Johari Window is considered, worldwide, to be a useful tool in examining oneself, becoming open-minded and improving that self-relationship.

The Johari Window

Created in 1955 by Joseph Luff and Harry Ingram, the Johari Window is considered a useful tool for understanding and learning various aspects of self. The window is also referred to as a disclosure and feedback model of awareness, so its use in Step Six becomes quite obvious as a tool to move forward.

In a Twelve-Step application, it could be used in the following way.

1. Open Area. The sponsor and sponsee choose attributes and characteristics that they both know about to fill in box one, the open area.

2. Hidden area. The attributes and characteristics that are known by the sponsee and not anyone else, populate box two – the hidden area. They may not be true or have any basis in fact, but if the sponsee thinks they are worth putting down then they are. Standard use of this tool says that it is up to the participant as to whether they disclose the contents of this box or not. In the context of Step Six, I think this is vital.

3. Blind area. This area represents information that the sponsee is not aware of but the sponsor perceives. Consideration for the sponsee and how to disclose this area to him/her should be taken.

4. Unknown area. Characteristics that have so far not been recognised go in this area. This may sound silly at first but this is the area of future development, of self-exploration, and of further consideration. This area requires the honesty and willingness that is mentioned at the beginning of Step Six in the *Twelve and Twelve*. The sponsee could, perhaps, look at the lists of thinking errors contained within this book

and spend some time in self-reflection, honestly appraising whether any of them are applicable or not. In my experience, this self-examination is a process that goes hand in hand with recovery and emerges as time goes by. The character defects I have today may not be the same ones I'm acting on a year from now.

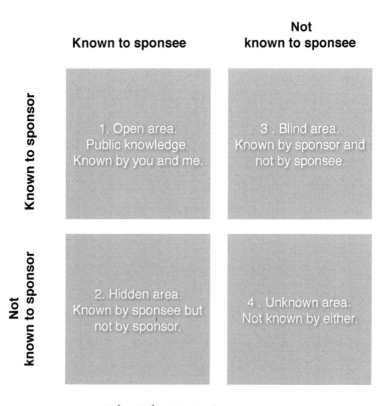

The Johari window

Character defects

The 'big book' identifies them and CBT identifies them. We all have ways of thinking that can be positive or negative. When these negative ways of thinking become barriers to healthy thinking they then interfere with decision-making, wise behavior, and relationships with others. In AA, these are referred to as character defects. Below is a list of thinking patterns that people in recovery will struggle with and people in active addiction will let run riot.

Grandiosity

Mentioned in the 'big book', grandiosity is the belief that a person is superior to others. A story, or point of view often shared, is that of a person lying in the gutter looking down on people. But what does that mean? When people were in the heights of their worse addiction and all was going wrong, perhaps they were filthy and smelly their warped perception still meant that they looked down on others as if those others were inferior even though they themselves were an absolute mess. I've heard many an example of people, say, sitting on their porch, drinking heavily and not achieving anything but who look crossly at their neighbour mowing the lawn or trimming the trees and think 'Loser. If only he had my life'. These thoughts can be persistent and when challenged, the person having the thoughts thinks that the challenger is obviously wrong to not be able to see life like him or her. While in this frame of mind, a person is unteachable because they know best.

Rationalisation (more)

While in addiction, people can rationalise the reasons for being the way they are. 'If you had my life you'd drink too', is a phrase that many will have heard. And, of course, the person saying those words absolutely believes them. People will seek explanations that sound plausible to others, and themselves, which can logically explain choices or decisions. Some of these may be quite pathetic and very obvious, from 'I went drinking because "Fred" asked me to', to the more complex and hidden types like, 'I drove the car while drunk because a friend of mine needed taking to the hospital'. People can (sometimes subconsciously) try to excuse themselves from the responsibility of their addiction, and this can extend to excusing themselves from all sorts of negative behaviors.

Minimising

Minimising is easy to do. So, you kissed the boss at the Christmas party, no big deal, you were drunk, and besides everyone does it. People try to take the power out of a disaster by belittling it. I often read of people being arrested for drink (or drug) driving and the statement that usually goes with it is that they were only JUST over the limit. (So, it doesn't really count.) This type of thinking reduces the blame to them self and can transfer it to someone else. In this case, 'I was driving perfectly OK. There was no need to stop me. I only got arrested because of the stupid breathalyser.' People can fool themselves into believing their own minimising. It beats feeling the remorse that goes with screwing up.

Blaming

Again, an easy error of thinking to fall into. It's easier to blame others than to take responsibility for ourselves. I can live with me if it's your fault. Further to that, people convince themselves, sometimes unintentionally, that an event or another person intentionally caused the problem and it's easier to blame that or them rather than take responsibility themselves. A really simple and maybe flippant example is a comment I've often heard: 'We ran out of milk so I had to go to the shop and get some. It's not my fault I ended up in the bar.' When probed on this sentence, the person giving it has on occasion confessed to throwing the milk down the drain so they had an excuse to leave the house. When you consider that that person's addiction may be destroying everything they have, you can see how powerful misdirected thinking can be.

Confusion

'Damn, someone is trying to tell me something that I need to hear and it's painful. I'll pretend I don't understand, and perhaps I'll convince myself of that. It will get me off the hook.' If people can feign a lack of understanding or confusion then they can break rules, disregard expectations, or avoid meetings. 'I didn't understand that the meeting was at 3 pm. Sorry I missed it. I must have got it confused with another time'. This person has diverted the responsibility by pretending they did not understand. Another example may be claiming not to remember or to be confused about how drugs came to be in their possession.

Assuming

A person can sometimes justify their own resentments, insecurities or paranoia by assuming, or pretending to assume, that they know what other people are thinking. They don't check out the facts by asking and can use this as an excuse to avoid the truth of a situation. It allows a person to behave badly without taking responsibility. A great example is that of a sponsee saying to the sponsor, 'I assumed you weren't going to the meeting tonight, so I didn't go either.'

Entitlement

Addiction is an illness that affects all levels of status, all walks of life, and all positions of employment. You can be extremely smart or not very clever and still end up with an addiction. A hindrance to recovery can be the feelings or belief of entitlement. Sometimes, in Twelve-Step meetings, you may hear the phrase 'Special and different' meaning that the believer doesn't think the rules apply to them. 'I'm not like any of you lot. I don't know why I'm here'. From the lawyer who decides he won't attend the group session in a rehab because 'what has someone as clever as me got to learn from those people', to the person in a meeting who looks at the Twelve Steps and can see why everyone else in the room should do them but can't (won't) relate it to themselves. Entitlement is a powerful roadblock that can hold people in their addictive behavior for years.

Another aspect of this may be the person who doesn't believe that they need to make amends for mistakes, won't admit their part in it, or believes they should be let off any consequences because of their status or who they are. Step Eight focusses on the willingness to make amends and this is a large part of the process of getting right-sized. Being humble is a powerful tool for having a self-awakening.

Lying

Perhaps lying doesn't take a lot of explanation since we all know what it is. Lying is used to bend the truth, avoid consequence, fool or make fools of other people, or omit mitigating factors. Tied in with denial, we hear the phrase 'you're lying to yourself'. It is a complex issue that may end up with judges and juries deciding on what is false or true. In active addiction, people can lie so often and about so much that they are easily found out because of the contradictions in their stories. Almost every person I know in recovery will admit to lying about their addiction at one point or another. 'Have you had a drink?' says one partner to another. 'Of course not,' says the other. Or 'I don't know how I got so drunk, someone must have spiked my drinks.' (All sorts of unhealthy thinking going on with this one).

What about the time people visit the doctors and when asked, 'How much do you drink?' reply 'Maybe a bottle of wine at the weekend.' Yes, lying is a major part of the dysfunctional thinking that goes with addiction, whether intentional or not.

Boredom

It's a great 'get out-of' line and you will see children use it often to get out of doing a chore that they don't wish to do. In addiction, as well as in other circumstances, adults can use this excuse to avoid all sorts of scenarios. Using the 'boring' excuse can often be a way of labelling something a person does not want to learn or engage with. It can give a person the excuse to look out of the window or put on the headphones. If it is boring or stupid then they don't have to deal with it. Instead of facing the problem or dealing with the issues, a person can act out in various destructive ways to hijack the event and hide from the areas that need to be addressed. 'So, why aren't you going to meetings?' asks the sponsor. 'Because they're all so boring,' replies the sponsee. (Meetings are anything but boring.)

Victim

'Poor me, poor me, **pour** me a drink' is a phrase that comes up in recovery groups and this attitude can be a part of victim thinking but often this is more about self-pity. In this context, the 'victim' is deliberately trying to control others by getting the other to feel sorry for them. Those crocodile tears will do wonders for making people back off. It's then easy to divest oneself of responsibility for the problems they have ended up with. 'The cruel world has done this to me and I'm not accountable!' may be what someone is really saying.

A point to mention here is the confusion some people have around attaching the use of the word 'powerless' in Step

One to victim thinking, which people can use to separate themselves from any responsibility for their behavior or choices. Being powerless over alcohol or addiction should not in any way be about divorcing oneself from the consequences of that addiction. However, many critics who have little understanding of the meanings of the steps can often highlight this error.

Side-tracking

Distracting people from the real issue is a great art that many a politician has managed to master. And like those whose thinking is at fault with this error, it can be very obvious or very subtle. Masters of it can control conversations, divert a question or just blatantly change the subject. People with addiction problems can use side-tracking to avoid subjects that make them uncomfortable and shifting the focus away from themselves into other areas. They may even be convinced that their own story is true.

Jealousy

Jealousy is a way of thinking that can be very destructive and it can manifest in several ways. For instance, the partner who seeks constant reassurance, people that constantly check where their partner is or follow their movements, people who set traps or tests for others, or the constant checking of a partner's phone. All of these will distract a person from their own recovery and can lead to angry retaliation for perceived wrongs in the relationship. Jealousy can be a self-fulfilling prophesy. Constantly checking on a loved one because you're scared of losing them can drive them away, so you lose them because of your own behavior. Retaliating for perceived wrongs strengthens the lack of trust on both sides of the relationship.

There are also some difficulties that arise in early recovery with jealousy. Not from the addict but from the partner. The intensity required in the first stages of recovery means that a partner can be neglected or feel left out. A couple of scenarios spring to mind. One is of the partner who feels abandoned and is angry that their husband/wife got sober but struggles with 'What was the point if he/she spends all their time at meetings now?' And the partner who feels betrayed and jealous because they have been trying to help their partner get well for years and now he/she is going to meetings and talking to complete strangers about it all... and it's working.

Search the internet and you will find many examples of 'roadblocks', 'thinking errors', 'cognitive distortions', and other ideas that limit a person's ability to get well. Surely understanding them will reduce the limitations on a person getting well.

Step Six conclusion

As in CBT, this Step is about recognising and listing those behaviors or character traits that are a hindrance to the sponsee. Most importantly, it's about those character traits becoming objectionable to the person who holds them. They need to discover how these defects get in the way of a peaceful life and what actions they can take to replace or stop them. If a person does not recognise that they do these things then perhaps the sponsor or therapist will be able to highlight episodes of dysfunctional thinking that are apparent to them. As in Step Five, it may be the role of an external person to shed some light on various situations.

Chapter Seven

Step Seven

'Humbly asked Him to remove our shortcomings.'

In this chapter, we will be looking at some of the skills, tools, and models that are recognised as being able to help a person learn new ways of thinking. A discussion heard throughout the world of abstinent recovery is one that goes along the lines of 'It wasn't enough to simply put down the drink or drug. Next, I had to learn how to live with me and live with life on life's terms.' Both CBT and the Twelve Steps recognise that ineffective personality traits, or shortcomings, need to be replaced with effective ones. Retraining oneself to act in different and positive ways is vital to change. By asking for help to remove shortcomings, a person is opening themselves up to new ways of thinking, whether that help is from a therapist, a group, sponsors, or higher powers.

Thinking skills

Behavior cycles are loops of behavior that keep repeating themselves and getting us into trouble or negative consequences. We are aware of some of these loops and even though we know they are bad for us we keep doing them anyway.

Some of these behaviors can be automatic, that is, we don't know that we are doing them. They are repeated again and again and we may be unaware that we are the cause of them.

Once we gain the opportunity to study our own cycles, they become easier to see and then become easier to change. Sometimes we need a sponsor or counsellor to raise our awareness of these patterns.

The keys to changing behavior cycles are awareness, honesty, and motivation. These are fundamental principles of Twelve-Step recovery, however, they may be reframed as Honesty, Open-mindedness, and Willingness or **HOW**. Let's go back to the principles of awareness, honesty, and motivation and explore them some more.

Honesty

Part of the progressive nature of Steps Six and Seven is the developing awareness that a person needs to have in order to identify and then challenge their own behaviors. Once they have developed the awareness then a degree of honesty is needed with which to tackle the defect. For instance, say I have become aware that I use too much bad language and that it offends some people. I can either carry on, pretending I don't care or that others are not offended, or get honest and admit to myself that I no longer like my own behavior and that I actually care about what others think of me. I shall, therefore, change my behavior.

In the *Twelve and Twelve,* under Step Six, a person reads about the nature of character defects in regards to self. How awareness grows, how sometimes people like to hold onto these behaviors, how some people's self-righteous behaviors and thoughts are enjoyable and they never want to change them. The focus is on becoming ready to have them removed.

In Step Seven, a person asks for them to be removed and therefore needs a great deal of self-awareness and skill to do this. They must be willing to admit to and recognise behavior cycles, which is not always possible. Sometimes, outside help is needed and this can take form in the role of sponsor or therapist. The sponsor, or a therapist, can act as devil's advocate, shining light onto areas a person is unwilling to look at. Again, this goes back to the trust and respect built up in that relationship and then the motivation to make those changes.

Open-mindedness

What of open-mindedness? Translated into CBT terms, these two words mean the opposite of rigid thinking, black-and-white thinking, or inflexibility. To have an open mind requires some effort and can be scary for many. It is surely one of the keys that opens the door to change.

Honesty and open-mindedness alone won't make the changes happen, self-will and determination are important too. In order to avoid lighting that next cigarette, avoid taking another drink, or complete that work you don't want to, a person will have to learn strategies and actions that will interrupt that cycle or behavior. Those thought patterns won't go away on their own; the subject must be willing to change and want to.

Willingness/motivation

Willingness is mentioned multiple times in Twelve-Step literature and so has considerable significance. It is, in this case, intricately tied in with motivation. We read of the willingness that is the foundation that can be built upon to achieve recovery. The willingness that is written about is an active condition driven by the motivation to change. It is about applying will in the right way, using this 'key' to repeatedly work hard at one's recovery, and apply self-will in the proper fashion while making right decisions and exerting oneself. Of course, the Twelve-Step approach is very wary of applying self-will and very much emphasises the need to align one's own will with that of a higher power. This attitude comes from a recognition that during active addiction, self-will is an absolute liability and, even in those early days of recovery, can sabotage any hope a person has of getting well.

Thought-stopping

There are some arguments that thought-stopping does not work. It is a strategy, however, as outlined here, and may be of help to people trying to 'stop' some of those shortcomings or character defects from happening. Thought-stopping is exactly what it sounds like. Every time you are aware of thoughts you don't want, or unwanted behaviors present themselves, you make a commitment to challenge your thoughts and redirect them. Saying 'Stop!' loudly (or in your head) to yourself, once you are aware of the thought, is the beginning of the process. You need to then replace it with an appropriate thought or action. One of the difficulties in early recovery is finding out what to replace those thoughts with and therefore we find the *Twelve and Twelve* expanding greatly on Steps Six and Seven compared to what was originally written in the 'Big Book' about these two steps. Sometimes, taking direct action can help a person. They may want to walk away from a situation, they might write a short inventory and perhaps, later, listen to some great music or visit the gym. A phrase that you will often hear around Twelve-Step meetings is 'Move a muscle, change a thought'.

An interesting part of Steps Six and thus Step Seven is the recognition that shortcomings and character defects present themselves as part of the journey. At first, a person may not know what these defects are, they don't know how to change them, or what form they take. CBT recognises the idea of retraining awareness so that a person develops into a position of self-awareness akin to these two steps. Working with anyone in the Twelve-Step arena we can see people, over a period of time, start to recognise the things that are causing them grief or anxiety. After a while, they then gain the ability to challenge them; this doesn't mean that they stop but that self-awareness is rising. After time passes and with the regular self-challenge and recognition of these shortcomings, the thoughts are stopped before they become behavior. They may even disappear altogether. This brings to mind the model of the four stages of competence, which has a similar learning curve.

Conscious Competence Learning Model

Recovery can be a tedious process for some expecting to know all the answers straight away and, as mentioned at the beginning of the book, have twelve months of recovery in six weeks. Learning, when in those early days, can be hard and arduous especially when we consider the process below, which is common to everyone when learning or attempting something new. As a person learns they go through the following levels:

Unconscious incompetence

The sponsee does not understand or know how to do something and may not recognise the defect. They may deny that there is a problem and not be conscious that it effects others, or maybe as it says in the *Twelve and Twelve,* they might enjoy the defect and prefer to hang on to it not knowing its impact on others. The individual must become conscious of his own shortcomings and the value of addressing them before moving on to the next stage. The length of time an individual spends in this stage depends on the strength of the stimulus to learn or, as mentioned in the 'big book', the amount of pain they are in.

Conscious incompetence

Though the persons do not understand or know how to change the shortcoming, they recognise the defect and the value of addressing it. They know what's wrong but still keep doing it. This is not an easy process, it can be extremely frustrating and mistakes will be made on the way.

Conscious competence

The sponsee knows what's wrong and how not to do it. This, however, takes a lot of concentration and energy, it takes a lot of practice and can feel quite challenging and draining. In the early days of recovery, this effort feels considerable to some and can develop into feelings of 'Is this really worth it?' People can sometimes slip back into autopilot when under stress and they need to be reminded that, as with any skill, practice is a necessary part of the process. Step Six and Seven remind people that even though we may strive for excellence we can only practice these things to the best of our ability - progress not perfection.

Unconscious competence

In the 'promises' after Step Nine, it is mentioned that 'we will intuitively handle things that used to baffle us' we have reached the level of unconscious competence. The skill has become second nature and the sponsee doesn't even have to think about doing it, even when completing other tasks. The individual is now in a position to teach it to others confidently, has a new inner confidence and is on the way to what AA describes as fourth-dimensional living.

Designing new core beliefs

We have previously explored core beliefs and how they set up a person's attitudes and perceptions of themselves. Step Seven is the point at which a person is trying to change things about themselves and changing those negative core beliefs has to be part of this process. CBT recommends the following ideas to initiate change in core beliefs.

- Be flexible. It's OK to get it wrong. 'I'm not responsible for my first thoughts.'

- Find alternatives. 'If this happens I will think that.' Look up a list of behaviors and feelings and the opposites, then when the destructive thoughts and beliefs occur practice the opposite.

- Look at the bigger picture. Explore the context of what went wrong and don't overgeneralise. For example, 'He looked at me funnily, therefore, everyone must hate me.'

When thinking about new ways of thinking, it may be wise to consider the popular acronym of SMART targets. There are a few different versions so I have chosen one that fits in with what we are trying to achieve.

S. Is it Specific? Do I really know what it is I want to change, or is it just a vague feeling?

M. Is it Measurable? How will I know if it's changed? What benchmark can I use?

A. What Action do I need to take to make it work?

R. Is it Realistic? Can I do it?

T. Is it Time-bound? What length of time am I going to allow myself to do this by?

It can be easy to say, 'Behave as you wish to be'. Some may look at this and figure it is just plain stupid. But, of course, there is merit in it as covered in the paragraph 'Fake it to make it'. Often in Twelve-Step circles, people are reminded that other people judged them by their actions and not their intentions. Many people can relate to this; remembering the days during active addiction, that even though full of love and respect for family and with absolutely no intention of hurting them, they did anyway. When asking to have shortcomings removed, if we don't start doing something about them ourselves, we are likely to be disappointed. Step Seven also requires effort on our part. Besides, if we are presenting a good front, even though that may be difficult, the positive feedback we get from others encourages us to succeed and thus we embed the new behavior and are no longer acting 'as if'.

Shortcomings vs character defects

I've heard mention of shortcomings and character defects being two ends of the same spectrum. It is worth exploring this concept and perhaps pondering on it. The theory goes like this: shortcomings are when a person does not have enough strength to complete something, stand by something, say no to someone, or push an idea through. A character defect is at the opposite end to this. A person is too pushy, wants to control everything, or won't take no for an answer.

These two ends of the spectrum are similar to the differences between being passive or aggressive. The passive person allows others to take control, might not stand up for themselves, and takes a stance of intimidation rather than resistance. The aggressive person is the one who demands, pushes through ideas regardless of consequence, and behaves like a bull in a china shop. Taking Step Seven literally, it would mean that only the shortcomings are the ones to be removed, but we know that this is just not true. A person wants to be rid of all of the things that will hinder recovery and a new life.

Step Seven conclusion

A person may see a clash here between the science base of CBT and the faith base of the Twelve Steps and they may be right. Step Seven is not, however, about lazing around doing nothing and waiting for a divine power to do all the work. It is about reaching out for help and finding the strength, solutions, and strategies to change those things that will not go away on their own. From both perspectives, CBT or Twelve Steps, this is about replacing dysfunctional personality traits with healthy ones. Both models recognise that this cannot be done in isolation.

Chapter Eight
Step Eight

'Made a list of persons we had harmed, and became willing to make amends to them all.'

Making lists and writing things down is commonplace in CBT. It enables people to focus on the task to be completed. Often set as homework assignments, CBT will direct people to consider the areas in their lives that they wish to improve upon and set them as goals. In a broad sense, these goals may be may be things like work, family, social situation, finance, and health, etc. Making amends, as in Step Eight, is a set of goals that when written down form the basis of a comprehensive plan of action that can now be worked on and, more importantly, be ticked off as completed.

In Step Eight, a person is looking at finding the willingness to move on from blame and anger towards others. I've heard mentioned that Step Eight is just a list, but to me, it is much more. The willingness that a person needs to find is a great deal bigger than just listing people. The list may be the start of the process but a large amount of soul searching, growing up, and tranquillity is needed for the willingness part. People should be trying to move away from the belief that their problems were someone else's fault. Of course, there may be instances where others were the cause and originators of difficult life events but this process is about forgiving and moving on. Both for oneself and for the other people.

Meanings attached to events

It seems glaringly obvious but the meanings we attach to events influence the way we respond to them emotionally. For example, a person goes to a great party where they are made to feel welcome and people are friendly. They have feelings of joy and happiness when remembering the event. Or a person attends a party that is hostile and unwelcoming. The person then attaches feelings of sadness or anxiety to the event. If you mention going to a party to either of these people then her reaction to you may be very different.(Remember this if someone is attending their first meeting. If they have a negative experience they may expect all meetings to be so).

During active addiction, a person may have built up many enemies or harmed many people but it may not be clear as to the true origins of the ongoing resentment, anger, or hostility towards that person. This takes time to work out. The meanings they have attached to events is automatic.

People don't stop and carefully examine a catalogue of potential explanations or meanings before having the emotions around an event. It happens very quickly without any thought. If those meanings are made when in active addiction, we can start to understand how they may be blurred or skewed, and in some cases may not exist at all. As a person's recovery progresses, they are more likely to see and understand the real facts of a situation and will be able to address the feelings that they have had around that 'person, place or thing' in a more productive way. As they say in CBT, 'feelings are not (always) facts'.

Hurt people hurt people

An error people can fall into is attaching the wrong meanings to events because they do not have the full picture or they make assumptions. 'Hurt people hurt people' is a phrase worth learning and can easily be applied to oneself or others. It can become a very circular state to get into, that is to say, that people can be defensive and awkward with you, reacting negatively or aggressively as a result of your behaving negatively or aggressively towards them at some time or other.

When people are hurt they tend to act out in the following ways.

1. They are quick to attack as a result of easily feeling threatened.

2. They misread others assuming others are against them.

3. They lash out and often can't see the harm they do.

4. They don't understand why others don't understand them.

5. They don't often let their guard down so always seem on the defensive.

6. They don't take responsibility for their own behavior.

7. They are easily offended.

8. They quickly turn to anger.

9. If feeling trapped, they will come out fighting.

10. They start to lose close friendships.

When a person becomes willing to make amends, they are part way along the journey of recognising that there are always two sides to the story. Those people who had been harmed during active addiction (or at any time) were hurt and will probably be resentful themselves. As it says in the *Twelve and Twelve*, it will take skill and time to be able to repair the harms of the past. Indeed, some of them may never be achievable.

Someone else's fault?

As in Step Four, a person needs to explore the concept of scapegoating and blaming others where there is no blame. Part of the willingness in Step Eight is about fact finding and becoming right-sized in regards to who was responsible for what. There are many sayings and phrases around blaming others or always playing the victim. In fellowship meetings, you will often hear people say that if 'there is one finger pointing out then there is always three pointing back', meaning that if you are always the victim or it's always someone else's fault then you had better look in the mirror. Step Eight is about changing the way a person looks at things. A radical shift in perception from blame to acceptance is needed. This calls into question the way a person has always looked at and dealt with things in the past. An examination of one's attitudes and beliefs is called for.

Steps Eight and Nine are also about repairing relationships and improving a person's relationships with every person they know. In order to do this, they have to move away from blame. Blame really means a person is choosing to avoid the problem and not address it or solve it. When a situation is someone else's fault, then a person doesn't have to do anything else about it nor do they need to understand it. It can be neatly packed away in a box as an unchangeable problem that someone else has responsibility for. It's easy to leave it there and hold onto the resentments, anger, or hostility towards others. This means that a person can ignore their part in it, either because it's too painful or because they can't bear the possibility that they might be responsible in some way, or even be wrong. Moving away from this thinking error will go a long way to help restore healthy, balanced and responsible thoughts.

Fake it to make it

In contrast to the above, there is some mileage in 'faking it to make it'. It is a small underlying principle of CBT used as a means to change behavior. It is also heard in Twelve-Step meetings, as is the phrase 'act as if'. So, does it really work? Obviously, caution needs to be exercised with this approach and we don't lead people into a state of pretence and make believe that sets up a state of dissonance within that person. There is, however, some good evidence to show that this works as found at the Mental Floss in their article '8 'Fake It 'Til You Make It' Strategies Backed by Science'. [1]

Number one argues that there is science to back up the belief that smiling lifts your mood.

Number two discusses evidence that the position we hold our bodies in affects the way we feel. People with a dominant pose have body chemistry changes that lead to them feeling more confident and positive.

Number three says that when we expect to know an answer we are more apt to get it right. If a person has negative beliefs that they are going to fail, or they think everyone thinks they are stupid and hang their heads low then they are indeed more likely to get it wrong than the person who has confidence and self-belief.

Number four concludes that the wearing of particular clothes is associated with certain qualities. As a reflection of this as regards addiction, we sometimes see people's personal standards and levels of hygiene drop as their illness progresses, and then when in recovery it creeps back the other way with people taking pride in their

[1] Amanda McCorquodale Feb 2016 *Fake it to make it.* Accessed 18 Jun 2018. http://mentalfloss.com/article/74310/8-fake-it-til-you-make-it-strategies-backed-science.

appearance and dressing well. We can also put on our party clothes to get in the party mood.

Listening to happy music is fifth on the list. It isn't hard to relate to this at all and often a tune will pick up a person's spirits when low, even if they were not seeking to be picked up.

Number six points towards the mimicking of good leaders. It says that if promoted, act as if you are someone who displays the skills. Even if you feel like a fraud you will open up your capacity to learn. In fellowship meetings, there are various applications of this with newcomers adopting behaviors modelled by people they admire or whose recovery they want.

As an example of actions leading to emotions, number seven discusses an experiment where people act as if they had romantic feelings for another. At the end of the experiment, they were more likely to want to see their experiment partner more than others who did not do the faking. Acting 'as if' can lead to genuine feelings.

Finally, number eight recognises that when a person enters a group, the way they portray them self on entry has a direct effect on their status within the group. Those who enter feeling confident and powerful would have an increase in status within the group. Not only during that first meeting but the effect would endure when subsequent meetings with the same group occurred.

'Acting as if' can be used as a form of role play and gives rise to the opportunity to practice alternatives to negative behaviors. When considering Steps Eight and Nine and making direct amends, it is recommended that a person starts with the easy ones first, this way one learns how to do them better. It might also be a good idea to do some role play with the sponsee (as often done in CBT), so that people are rehearsed and confident when it comes to the real situation. Perhaps the sponsor could take on several stances ranging from devil's advocate to overly friendly. As with any skill, people need to practice it in an easier situation first and gain competence before trying to apply it to trigger situations.

Pretending is not always good

With the CBT approach, it is advised to remember that positive thinking models should be genuine and not just a form of pretending that all is OK. What does this mean? It can be self-defeating and unhealthy to act warm and friendly to another when deep inside the person your acting friendly toward is really loathed. This will set up conflict inside oneself and can lead to unbearable tension.

Further to this, if a person pretends all is jolly and good to the outside world but on the inside they are falling apart and are suppressing how they really feel, problems can arise. This can lead to an eventual situation where a person believes they have failed based on their observation of others, they see everyone else being happy and assume that they are, but don't yet feel it themselves, they feel like a fraud and as if they are the only one struggling. 'I'm the only one who can't get this,' they say and so give up.

Step Eight conclusion

Active addiction leaves many casualties along the way. To quote the 'Big Book', 'The alcoholic is like a tornado roaring his way through the lives of others'. There has been plenty of damage done. Step Eight is one of the tools necessary for the reconstruction of relationships, both with self and others and for the repair of damage vital for the tranquillity needed for long-term recovery.

Chapter Nine

Step Nine

'Made direct amends to such people wherever possible, except when to do so would injure them or others.'

Making direct amends can be considered similar to the behavioral assignments that may be undertaken in CBT. It is a way of practising and testing out new behaviors, which can lead to new beliefs based on the outcome of those new behaviors.

Restoration

There are some cautions advised, which are mentioned below, but on the whole, it is well-known that when people take steps to make amends the person injured is more likely to forgive and forget. In fact, this is so widely recognised as a healing process, we have criminal justice systems set up to pursue this very practice. Studies show that this works and the psychological processes at play generate forgiveness.

Remember, though, this is not just about the injured person. For damaged relationships to survive, people need to heal and this may mean that the person who caused the damage has to do a lot of hard work to repair a relationship. Often, the sponsee feels a lot more confident about their progress and state of forgiveness than the person on the other end. Repeated promises of change and then repeated relapses make family members sceptical and it takes a long time for forgiveness and trust to build up or return. As it says in the 'big book', 'there is a long period of reconstruction ahead'. A person also needs to remember that if a long time has passed since needing to make the amends, then a process of procrastination can evolve where it is easier just to pretend the whole thing never happened. The underlying pain of this 'intentional ignoring' can take its toll leading to hidden feelings of stress or anxiety.

Check the ecology

In Neurolinguistic Programming (NLP), the term 'ecology' refers to the impact on the overall life of the client and those around them following a course of action. This is vital when ascertaining whether a goal is valid or not. Similarly, with Step Nine, people should consider the same; what will be the impact on themselves or those to whom the amends are made.

There are two vital issues to check for:

1. Validity: is the goal a true and positive outcome or an false one that will worsen the situation?

2. Ecology: will attaining the goal cause side effects for the client or those around them?

This therapy-based approach has been a consideration of Step Nine since its creation. Focusing on the ecology of the situation, as per point two above, we can clearly see that Step Nine's wording 'except when to do so would injure them or others' is very considerate of the possible side effects that making amends could cause.

If the ecology is checked, or the sponsor looks at the amends to be made and finds them to be 'at risk', then this means that whatever amends are listed will have a negative side effect for either the sponsee, or those around them, and they need to be made in a different way.

If the ecology is unsound, or the amends too damaging, a person does not have to simply abandon the step. Instead, the amends can be broken down into manageable parts with the goal being to find an alternative or safer way of making them. A person always needs to make amends with support and guidance from others, whether that be sponsor or therapist. Two examples below show how sometimes things can go wrong and the amend, perhaps, should not be pursued.

1. Example one is of an ex-boyfriend, who some fifteen years after splitting up from a girlfriend decides to get in touch to make amends. She is now married and has moved on from the trauma of the damaging relationship. By getting in touch, he has opened up old wounds and alerted the new husband to a period of her life that she had put behind her.

2. Example two is of a group guys were arrested when making amends for shoplifting that they did many many years ago. Putting them in jail will cost the taxpayer heavily, will threaten their recovery, and achieve very little. I'm not saying that there crimes should go unpunished but that the consequences of making the amends were pretty negative for all.

Time-machine thinking

We have all done it. 'If only I had said this' or 'If only I hadn't done that', I wouldn't be in this situation now. We can 'regret the past' but must learn to move on from it. As it says in the part of the 'big book' that has become commonly known as the promises people can achieve a state of mind on completion of Step Nine that is of 'not regretting the past' nor 'wishing to shut the door on it'. It does take some time to move on from hanging on to past events or moving away from the power they have over you. The pain of early recovery is often surrounded by blame and anger and it takes a while to understand why some people may say that they are a 'grateful recovering alcoholic' because 'what the hell is there to be grateful for?'

This thinking will shift and part of that is coming to terms with the past. A starting point can be to understand that you categorically cannot change the past. Think about it, if you went back in time and told yourself not to drink that next pint, or smoke that other joint would you listen. You wouldn't listen to anyone else so what makes you think you'd listen to yourself? We can apply this to many situations but the truth of the matter is we can't change a thing and had better get used to it. A strange effect that seems to happen is that people do start to remember things in the past differently. Blame reduces and anger softens as people see their past in a different light.

In both CBT and when working the Steps, there can be some stumbling blocks. People may feel that all the planning and talking about the actions they are going to take fall apart when crunch time comes (in this case applying Steps Eight and Nine). They react or think they will, with their old behaviors or on their old fears, even when they don't want to. CBT and the Twelve Steps remind us that with any skill, practice is the key. Step Nine recommends a person makes amends starting with easy ones and work their way up.

Communication

Communication, of course, is vital to every walk of life, but in Step Nine, we can give it some focus. The 'big book' and *Twelve and Twelve* give people direction on making amends, recommending that starting with the easier ones is a good place to begin. For some, this will require some practice and self-awareness, which may not come easy. People will need to consider their communication skills. How do they talk to people? As human beings, we often make the same mistakes when it comes to talking to others and below we have a list of communication barriers.

- We assume people know what we are talking about.

- We assume people know what we are feeling.

- We don't listen well.

- We sometimes overreact to what people say.

- We are not always clear about saying 'No'.

In preparation for making direct amends in Step Nine, people should be encouraged to examine which parts of the list above apply to them and take action to counteract them.

This leads on to three communication styles that can make or break a conversation. Is a person passive, assertive, or aggressive?

Learning from the following examples can be of benefit when considering how to talk to others when making amends.

- Passive style: Stutters and stumbles over words and looks down at feet. Says, 'I'm really sorry I was so awful. It's all my fault. I'll do whatever you want to make up for it.'

- Assertive Style: Makes friendly direct eye contact looks relaxed. Says, 'I'm making amends for my behavior as part of my Twelve-Step programme. Can I begin with...'

- Aggressive Style: Overbearing and invading of body space. Says, 'Listen, you schmuck. I'm making amends and you'd better like them.'

We can see from the examples above that it may take a bit of practice to get it right, especially when nerves are running high and people feel pressured in these situations.

Step Nine conclusion

The rewards of making amends are many. Not only will it increase positive feelings of happiness but this step will also increase self-confidence and self-esteem, which are a vital part of any treatment or therapy. If a person is genuine in their amends, that is to say, they are not just apologising, then the outward ripple effect will help them in their standing in the community and places of work. Steadfast growth and proving one's determination to others are very important. However, it may take a while for others to believe that the change is permanent.

Chapter Ten
Step Ten

'Continued to take personal inventory and when we were wrong promptly admitted it.'

Maintaining change

Self-awareness is an important part of maintaining change and of being able to take personal inventory. Below is a list of healthy ideas to help with Step Ten.

Open thinking

- Be open to ideas, views and perceptions of others.

- If a person reacts defensively or in anger when they hear or read something that challenges their beliefs, remind them that they might be overlooking an idea that could help them.

- Practice acceptance of positive criticism.

- Listen with interest to the ideas of others; a person may learn something.

- Look for the similarities, not the differences.

Accept personal responsibility

- People should own up to mistakes in thinking and behaviors rather than dodging them.

- People must learn not to try to and lay their mistakes on someone else. Once they are able to do this, they are on the road towards changing their life for the better.

Develop a realistic self-view.

- Remind people that everyone you know makes mistakes.

- Part of Step Ten is learning to recognise mistakes, seeing what happened, and owning the parts of it that are relevant. Discussing what happened with another and trying to learn any lessons that they can see. By taking this action, a person improves their chances of not repeating them and reinforces their recovery.

- Reassure people that mistakes do not make them worthless.

Analyse your performance.

- People should learn to actively examine their performance on a daily basis. This ties in with Steps Four, Ten and Eleven.

- The importance of making yourself accountable for your own behavior is a vital part of being able to maintain recovery as mentioned above. But analysing it takes it a little further.

- If a behavior is decent and proper then people will have less to resent about them self, if anything at all. They can, therefore, hold their heads up high and be proud of who they are. This is not to say that if they do make mistakes they should live in shame. Remember that recovery is a journey and it takes continued effort on a daily basis to shift away from old behaviors.

Consider consequences.

A person may feel that recovery is going to be 'dull, boring, and glum' and they may seek the thrill or excitement of their previous life. If tempted to engage in risky behavior or take part in an exciting activity, take time to stop and consider the consequences. If the outcome of your behavior is negative, e.g., you end up in trouble with the police, then your chances of relapse are higher. Likewise, if the outcome of your behavior leaves you on an incredible high you may forget you are in recovery and pick up a drink. This is not to say you shouldn't have fun but that recovery must always be at the heart of your life.

Face your fears

A great book written by Susan Jeffers is *Feel the fear and do it anyway*. There are a great many fears that people bring into their recovery with them and often they have no basis in reality. Sometimes, however, they are very real indeed. In recovery, you can learn to challenge those irrational fears and move through them, or even learn how to overcome the real fears and achieve in areas that you thought were never possible. Remember to always check with another and discuss these fears and not to rush in where angels fear to tread – the safety of your recovery is the most important thing.

Let go rather than needing to control.

Recognise that you do not need total power and control over every event and every person. Stop trying to force or persuade others into doing what you want. Twelve-Step groups use the serenity prayer to remind themselves of this: 'God grant me the serenity to accept the things I cannot change, the courage to change the things I can, and wisdom to know the difference.'

First thoughts

People aren't responsible for their first thoughts and so need to learn to deal with them accordingly. There are many situations that people can have guilt and shame around that they are not responsible for. Ever been followed by a police car and felt as if you must have done something wrong? These feelings pop into your head even when you have nothing to hide. You are not responsible for them but you are responsible for what you do with them. If you were to hit the gas and try to run from the police then you would end up in a lot of trouble, just because you had a thought.

When a person has thoughts that are not premeditated – those very first thoughts that can jump into consciousness without permission – they are not responsible for them. People need to learn that when they criticise others, or immediately get a resentment or feel anger or despair then they have a chance of changing those feelings and thoughts. CBT recognises that what we think we feel and if we change our thinking then we change our feelings. If a person learns to stop, take a breather, and re-examine their thoughts then they can move on from them or change direction. In AA, people often talk about starting the day over, a concept they had never thought of before, and this gives them permission to move on, not dwell, and have a brighter day.

Experiments are recommended along the lines of letting yourself off the hook, e.g. when someone pulls in front of you in traffic, your first thoughts may not be very polite, let yourself off the hook – it's OK – pause and have a rethink, count to ten or say the Serenity Prayer. People will start to feel freer and more peaceful as they get better at exercises like this and realise that they can be responsible for the thoughts that follow thoughts. This brings us onto ANTs.

Automatic negative thoughts - ANTs

Again, repeating from the last topic, most people's thoughts happen automatically. This means that they generally don't have to work hard to perform their activities of daily living. It's a good thing. People who are depressed – and alcohol is a depressant – can find themselves thinking about the world and the future in a negative way. This way of thinking is known as Automatic Negative Thoughts and in my experience is empowered greatly because of a person's addiction. Often diagnoses of depression are handed out on a plate when the real driving issue is the primary problem of addiction, which pushes these negative automatic thoughts.

So how can they be identified and what are the characteristics?

1. **They are always negative**. A person misses a phone call that was arranged and therefore thinks they are useless. They don't ever do anything right and others just always think they are idiots.

2. **They are automatic**. They just seem to come into a person's thoughts without any effort. A person does not choose to have them and they are very difficult to stop.

3. **They can be distorted**. They are not always supported by evidence or by what a person knows to be true.

4. **They are unhelpful.** They keep a person in a negative mindset and feeling depressed, this makes change very difficult.

5. **They are plausible.** The person that has them accepts them as valid and does not question them.

The more depressed a person becomes, or the longer they drink to excess, the more of these types of negative thoughts they have, and the more they believe them. This type of thinking forms a vicious circle; the more you drink the more negative thoughts you have, the more you believe them the more depressed you become so you drink more and round it goes.

Seemingly irrelevant decisions (SIDs)

I remember many years ago a therapist talking to me about SIDs and dismissing her ideas as nonsense. I believed then a person is always in control and always makes decisions based on incredibly judgement and skill. I have since found out that this is not always true (if ever). This decision-making process is often connected to relapse as a direct contributor when looked at in hindsight. So, what is it?

Possibly a form of self-sabotage, SIDs occur when a person chooses to do something that puts their recovery at risk but does not see the connection. Easy examples are found like visiting a friend who lives next door to a bar. Going to the supermarket with no real plan and finding oneself walking down the booze aisle. Carrying more money than necessary is a common trap.

Fellowship meetings have several sayings that highlight the type of thinking involved in SIDs. For instance, 'If you go to the barber's for long enough, you'll end up with a haircut.' The 'big book' reminds people to only attend places if they have a legitimate reason for doing so, and then they should have a well-thought-out escape plan. Raising the awareness of this type of thinking is good for the newcomer who, once aware, starts to take considered responsibility for the actions they take.

The Superman Effect

Over the years I have witnessed many people relapse around the Six-to-twelve-weeks mark. What goes on? Addiction is a cunning foe that tells a person they are alright and it will be different next time. After a few weeks without alcohol or drugs, their body starts to feel better, they can think without pain, they don't shake anymore or have horrible sweats, they wake up naturally and feel good, their family or friends appreciate their company, and they feel as if they've got it all worked out. Their thoughts lie to them and say that they can just have one drink or a quick smoke and they will be alright, it will be different this time. The mental obsession with drugs or alcohol has not left them yet. They feel like Superman. They can take on the world and everything will be alright. 'I've got this,' they say to them self. They pick up a drink or a drug and it all goes horribly wrong yet again. They relapse. Some don't ever make it back.

Taking inventory

In the *Twelve and Twelve,* the term spiritual axiom is used, referring to the idea that every time a person is emotionally disturbed, 'no matter what the cause', there is something wrong with them. The disturbance is internal and the person owns that disturbance. It goes on to highlight that even if circumstances mean that feelings like anger are justified or appropriate to that situation, these feelings are dangerous to those recovering as they will put them closer to a drink. Justified or not those struggling to find recovery or even those in long-term recovery, need to work out that it matters little whether they are entitled to those feelings or not. Those feelings or emotions will ultimately only hurt them. Taking a self appraisal (or inventory) can be of help.

There are five types of inventory identified in Step Ten.

1. The spot-check inventory.
   The Twelve-Step approach here is to sensibly analyse what is involved in the situation, recognise ownership of the fault, have a willingness to forgive (self and others) looking for slow and steady change in the situations and not a miraculous turnaround.

2. At the end of the day.

   Compile a balance sheet of the day looking for the good parts and the bad and examine the motives behind these situations. It is also recommended that people try to visualise what might have been done better and what they did well.

3. A progress review.

   It is recommended that people review their progress with either their sponsor or a trusted other. A common tool in CBT.

4. An annual or semi-annual house cleaning.

   Many people in Twelve-Step recovery will revisit Steps Four and Five. Recovery is progressive and a person's beliefs and ideas about them self and their own behaviors will change over time. Memories can surface later in the journey that had been repressed or forgotten and so a visit to these Steps is not a bad idea.

5. The occasional retreat.

   Retreats are a place to get away from it all, time to recharge the batteries, or a place to relax, meditate, study mindfulness or other such healing techniques. These are not just common to AA but to people from all walks of life. Many AA people find this of real benefit.

So, what is the CBT equivalent to taking inventory? When it comes to challenging thought processes there is a combination of methods that can be used. These methods will bring the errant thoughts into consciousness so they can be examined and new outcomes can then be sought. Thought forms can be created using the below headings depending on the situation, these headings are similar to the headings covered in Step Four but there are some variations. They are not dissimilar to the Twelve-Step approaches written above.

1. **When?**

   What time did it happen? Is there a pattern?

2. **Why?**

   What was the situation?

3. **How?**

   How did you get into the situation? Or how did it arise?

4. **Who?**

   Who were you during the incident, what role were you playing?

5. **Who else?**

   Who else was involved? What was their part in it?

6. **Really why?**

   Is this an honest appraisal? Can you see the truth in it?

7. **Options?**

   What choices do you have now?

8. **New way?**

   How will you do this in the future?

9. **Feedback?**

   Can I get feedback from friends or a trusted other? Out of ten, how would you score the situation in terms of success or difficulty?

Drinking Dreams and Emotional Hangovers

Understanding a person's dreams (as mentioned at the beginning of the book) has value in the fact that it may lead to a deeper understanding of one's fears and anxieties. Maybe it's the thoughts and ideas that have been running around in the subconscious that are causing the person's issues.

In the case of drinking or using dreams, there seems to be an obvious connection to the angst around those days of using or drinking. Those hidden or obvious anxieties sometimes manifest themselves in dreams that are full of fear, cause internal conflict, and are downright scary. People can wake from these dreams feeling extreme guilt and anxiety. They can sometimes take a while to realise that the dream was not real and that they did not relapse. Powerful stuff. Anyone who is not in recovery or has not experienced such a dream should recognise the impact that they may have on not just someone in their early days but anyone who experiences such powerful episodes. These dreams can leave people with an emotional hangover, that is to say, that they feel the negative emotions of anger, fear, jealousy, etc. as the result of a night when their head just wouldn't seem to relax and shut up.

Emotional hangovers, as mentioned above, are those times when a person feels anger, fear, jealousy, and other painful emotions as a result of being unable to move on from, or being caught up in, negative thoughts, behaviors, and beliefs. Feeling miserable today because of the misdemeanours of yesterday is quite common. As a strategy, living 'just for today' need not only apply to drinking or using but also to letting go of painful or emotional stuff that happened yesterday. There is real evidence for emotional hangovers and indeed New York University researchers have concluded that emotional experiences can induce 'physiological and internal brain states' that persist for a long time after the emotional event has ended. [2]

Step Ten has a focus on taking inventory and, when wrong, promptly admitting it. CBT has some similar concepts around identifying the behaviors, thoughts, and emotions that a person wants to change. The starting point is being able to identify what it is that needs changing. It's often difficult in early recovery for a person to identify what feelings they are actually having and whether they are healthy or unhealthy. Many CBT books will have tables or lists of emotions and feelings to help with the identification process. Making the link between thoughts, behaviors, and where a person applies their attention will be a focus of CBT and is the key to getting well.

When someone is aggressive and angry with you do you then behave in any of the following unhealthy ways?

1. Go out and get drunk?

2. Beg for forgiveness when it wasn't your fault?

---

[2] New York University. "Is there such a thing as an emotional hangover? Researchers find that there is." ScienceDaily. ScienceDaily, 26 December 2016.www.sciencedaily.com/releases/2016/12/161226211238.htm

3. Make promises that you may or may not be able to keep?

4. Make a decision to never interact with that person again?

The above responses are generally not healthy and can often come about when feeling guilty, depressed, shameful, or fearful. It may take another person to point out that you are responding that way when there are healthier or more positive options. The four points below are the alternate to the four points above:

1. Feel uncomfortable but don't run away from the situation.

2. Apologise for your part in it.

3. Recognise the situation as a learning point and reassure others that you will try not to do it again.

4. Recognise the 'attacker' as a sick person whom sometimes has anger issues. It's not personal.

So, the focus is on the reality of the situation rather than the emotions and the fear they generate, which can often result in some sort of self-punishment – conscious or unconscious.

Let's look at the situation again but from a 'focus' point of view. Someone is aggressive and angry with you, and you are in a place where guilt, depression, shame, or fear are hanging over you. You put the focus unfairly on yourself. Do you:

1. Blame yourself for them being angry, i.e., 'It's always my fault anyway'?

2. Feel so overwhelmed with the pain of it all that you can't see a solution or any way out?

3. Start to collude with the attacker and seek evidence that it was 'your fault'?

4. Start to think that everyone else is blaming you as well?

With this negative focus, you are heading into that state mentioned earlier of an emotional hangover. You continue to beat yourself up long after the situation is done and dusted.

Daily focus

An interesting element of CBT, which fits straight in with Step Ten, is the awareness of the need to focus our attention on the negative aspects of the day. If a person doesn't respect, understand, and resolve the things that are creating problems then how can they improve on them, move on from them, and avoid the situations in the future?

CBT recommends the following three important stages.

1. **Acknowledge the problem**, respect it and make a resolve to deal with it at the appropriate time. I often remind people that Step Ten says 'promptly admitted it' rather than 'immediately admitted it' and why is this? For me, it fits in with this part of CBT that says learning to deal with things at the appropriate time moves us towards a position of not being dominated by it. It will also help us from rushing in like a bull in a china shop or exacerbating a situation and making it worse.

2. **Change the state.** This means making a conscious decision not to dwell on the issue but focus on something positive instead. This is not dismissing the situation but gives a person permission to put the problem on hold and return to it later when in a better emotional place.

3. **Remember to deal with it.** This is a good prompt to do a daily inventory in the evening and find time to come back to the issue and resolve it. This is also helpful in rebuilding self-trust and self-efficacy. If

problems are too big then the nature of Twelve-Step fellowships means that there is always someone on the end of a phone who a person can chat with.

Step Ten is not about beating oneself up and constantly taking inventory as if it's a religious path to freedom. The 'big book' reminds people that taking inventory in red ink – only focusing on negatives – is not a true reflection of one's day.

Step Ten conclusion

The need to monitor ongoing actions and behaviors is clear when it comes to developing an awareness of the potential of backwards progress.

If, when a person becomes able to recognise that they are moving closer to old behaviors or old thinking, they can interrupt the process and take corrective action, then they are successfully applying the principles of CBT and Step Ten. At first, in person's journey, this is best done with a journal. Later on, in recovery, people become aware that this practice has become so embedded that they can complete their daily inventory mentally without the use of a journal. Some people continue to use journals for the rest of their lives and some people revert to writing the journal when they are having a little difficulty in life. They wish to refocus on their daily inventory and find that reverting to writing it helps a great deal. Using the ABC method covered in Step Two is a cognitive approach to helping this daily process.

Chapter Eleven

Step Eleven

'Sought through prayer and meditation to improve our conscious contact with God as we understood Him, praying only for knowledge of His will for us and the power to carry that out.'

Psychology and the Serenity Prayer

Amy Butcher PhD writes about the Serenity Prayer, (the well-known prayer made particularly famous by its use in AA) as being a cross between Acceptance and Commitment Therapy (ACT) and CBT. She says that if there is something you cannot change then ACT will help you to accept it. If there is something you can change then CBT will give you the tools and courage to try. Many people all over the world use this prayer regularly and it means different things to different people depending on when and why they use it. For instance, many Twelve-Steppers use the prayer when:

- Angry with someone

- When feeling stressed and under pressure

- Prior to an event

- When frustrated and feeling powerless

- When wanting a bit of courage to tackle something

- When needing to ground oneself

- As part of a meditation

- To reach out to God or a higher power

So, we see that the therapeutic advantages of using prayer can be quite important.

Prayer

There is no set way to pray and the Twelve Steps say that you should have a God of your own understanding. Consequently, prayer is personal. Many recovering people have found that when they get down on their knees and prayed, their whole attitude changes and they feel free and uplifted rather than subservient and less than. Some people believe prayer works because of that link with God or a higher power and some believe it works as a cognitive tool to direct and focus thinking. Its up to you which one you believe.

People can also use prayer throughout the day when they find themselves in difficult situations. Many people like to use the Serenity Prayer in tough situations as a lifebelt to help them through. It can give you enough time to take the edge off of an otherwise overpowering situation.

Meditation

It takes a while to learn how to relax and meditate. Most people in early recovery will relate to the inability to quieten or 'shut their heads up'. They will understand when you talk about sitting, trying to be still and quiet, when – all of a sudden – your head has hit the spin-dry cycle (like on a washing machine) and you are thinking of everything apart from being still and quiet. It is important to remind people that their concentration will wander, they will have intrusive thoughts, and meditation or relaxation takes practice. If a person finds their concentration wanders or they do have intrusive thoughts tell them not to worry and just remind them they can draw themselves back into the exercise and start at the last point they can remember. This is natural.

Relaxation

In order to meditate, a person needs to relax. There are a number of recognised advantages from the use of regular relaxation techniques, one of which is meditation. It is also considered that depression and anxiety cannot coexist within a state of guided relaxation.

During the state of relaxation, the following apply:

- Breathing slows down

- Muscles relax

- Blood pressure levels fall to natural 'resting' levels

- Heart rate becomes slow and regular

- Background sounds will often appear to fade as they become a lesser priority

- Adrenaline levels fall and endorphin levels tend to increase, reducing pain and tension and creating a sense of healing and well-being

- Visualisations get stronger

- The conscious mind relaxes

- Memories can improve

Further to this, relaxation can help:

- Someone calm down if they feel tension rising

- Reduce physical and mental stress levels

- Create pauses in the day so, may be good to operate, work from home

- Speed up recovery after sporting activities

- Provide a space for spiritual connection

- Guide a person towards positive thinking.

When attempting to relax or meditate, it may be of help to set up a relaxing routine that a person can associate with doing relaxation. This is often a good thing to do before going to bed when the rest of the household is quiet.

Simple relaxation techniques

Don't use the exercises in any environment where for health or safety reasons you need to concentrate fully on another task, e.g. when driving.

Counting backwards

Close your eyes and then breathe in slowly and deeply, filling your lungs.

Breathe out slowly and calmly.

In your thoughts, repeat the number you started from.

Continue counting backwards using this process until you have reached zero.

Don't set yourself too high a number you may not be able to keep this up on a regular basis. It is better to build from a low starting point than to set yourself a target that you are unlikely to keep.

To prepare for each exercise, a person would normally find somewhere comfortable, where they will not be disturbed and sit or lie in a position that they find relaxing.

Tensing your toes

Close your eyes and focus your attention on your toes.

Curl your toes up tightly, but not so much it hurts.

Slowly count to ten.

Relax your toes.

Slowly count up to ten again.

Repeat steps two to five as often as you like but a minimum of five times.

Relaxing imagination

Shut your eyes and imagine yourself in a place that you find enjoyable; a relaxing place that is stress-free. (This will vary from person to person depending on what they like as an individual.) You could be in a wood, by a lake, or at the beach, or in your favourite place of all time. Whatever situation you choose, make sure it is calm, relaxing, and worry-free. Once you are there, try to imagine it in as much detail as you can.

What sounds can you hear?

What things can you see?

Who else is there?

What can you smell?

How does your body feel?

After the time you allowed for the session, open your eyes and resume your normal activities ensuring that you are fully awake. Set a time limit.

Guided meditations can be great if a person finds the right one for them. This may take some experimentation and a little perseverance. I've listened to guided meditations and relaxation CDs that did the complete opposite of relax me. The speaker's voice got on my nerves, the background noises were annoying to me (the birds tweeting randomly drove me to a state of distraction), or I just didn't like the mood-setting music. I did learn that taking action to find a technique that suited me was important and that it took some effort. However, this is vital when pursuing recovery.

Step Eleven, and the ability to learn how to relax, take a breath, and refocus ultimately connects with all the other Steps but in particular Step Ten. It is of great advantage if, when a person takes inventory, does a spot check or considers they have done something wrong or made an error, that that person can look at the situation in a relaxed and non-anxious way. The picture will be a lot clearer if not clouded by fear or out-of-balance emotions.

Morning and nightly affirmations

The Step-Eleven concept of morning and nightly prayer and concentrating on the positives of the day ahead is a great form of positive affirmation. The 'big book' suggests that in the morning, a person starts the day by thinking of the hours to come, thinking of the day's work, and the opportunities to be helpful. In the same way, CBT recommends starting the daily routine with positive affirmations. A simple suggestion is to write down clearly areas to improve upon but write them in a way that becomes an affirmation. For instance, if you feel that an area to be improved is that you don't make eye contact with people or smile, your affirmation may say, 'I smile and make eye contact with people.' The idea is to keep it simple and write four things to be aware of and improve. Ask the person to carry them with them and look at them several times and repeat them out loud. Many people in Twelve-Step recovery do a similar exercise with something called the 'Just for Today' card. A set of positive affirmations written on a card that many carry on themselves. The CBT proposal is that a person also reads through the card, or affirmations at night when feeling sleepy and just about to nod off. While in this sleepy state, CBT puts forward the idea that our brains are more susceptible to suggestion.

Step Eleven conclusion

Meditation and relaxation techniques are recognised throughout the world as an important part of being human. The spiritual element of what it means to be a person is also gaining strength in the medical world. This understanding of the need for self-contentment, the need for peaceful and quiet thoughts, and the ability to tap into a spiritual element of the universe – whatever that be – is a model that clinicians are starting to believe in more and more. We need to be reminded that we are not robots but are deeply emotional beings who absolutely need a sense of connection with others and the world in order to find something resembling tranquillity.

Chapter Twelve

Step Twelve

'Having had a spiritual awakening as the result of these steps, we tried to carry this message to alcoholics and to practice these principles in all our affairs'

Spirituality

The spiritual side of recovery is starting to be taken seriously. It is mentioned in the recent definition of addiction by ASAM: 'Addiction is a primary, chronic disease of brain reward, motivation, memory and related circuitry. Dysfunction in these circuits leads to characteristic biological, psychological, social and **spiritual** manifestations.' The definition goes on to say that there are other factors that can contribute to the appearance of addiction and one of them is, 'Distortions in a person's connection with self, with others and with the transcendent (referred to as God by many, the Higher Power by Twelve-Steps groups, or higher consciousness by others)'.

The book *Recent Developments in Alcoholism, Vol 18* introduces itself with the following description:

'It was once taken for granted that peer-assisted groups such as Alcoholics Anonymous had no "real" value in recovery from addiction.' More recently, evidence-based medicine is recognising a spiritual component in healing— especially when it comes to addiction. The newest edition of *Recent Developments in Alcoholism* reflects this change by focusing on the Twelve-Step model of recovery as well as mindfulness meditation and other spiritually oriented activity.

AA highlights that there is a difference between a spiritual experience and a spiritual awakening. The first is a vast change in feeling and outlook as the result of 'sudden and spectacular upheavals' that have a religious, or 'God' context. The second is described as an awakening of the educational kind; a slow and progressive shift in attitudes and reactions to life. Study hard enough and you will find examples of both all over the world. It doesn't matter whether you believe in the 'spiritual' element of this step or not. What does become clear is that people have a profound shift in attitude, strength, and the ability to cope with life without drugs or alcohol. As it says in the *Twelve and Twelve*, 'the most important meaning of it is that he has now become able to do, feel and believe that which he could not do before'. This is exactly what CBT tries to achieve. To quote Mind, the UK's leading mental health charity that helps millions of people, 'In CBT, you work with a therapist to identify and challenge any negative thinking patterns and behavior, which may be causing you difficulties. In turn, this can change the way you feel about situations, and enable you to change your behavior in future'.

Externalising

Step Twelve recognises the benefits of helping others but we need to be aware of the dangers of 'externalising'. This is when a person can't cope with their own issues so is fixated on helping or controlling others thus avoiding their own issues. By focusing on others, they steer clear of facing their own demons and in turn, this makes them feel stronger and better. They may come across as an AA guru or seem to be leading the way in recovery and at meetings. It can be difficult to tell the difference between those who are genuinely kind, helpful, and in the know and those who are compensating by avoiding issues about self. An indicator may be that they broadcast how wonderful they are and give a sense of needing followers.

In AA, there is a phrase called 'two stepping'. This is when a person is only working Step One and Step Twelve and this comes with a warning. Putting a lot of effort into helping others, which can be commendable, can come at a price of neglecting one's own self-development. Recovery can become dull and a person feels discouraged. If someone is then faced with a personal crisis they may not have the tools to deal with it and remain in recovery.

There are still tremendous benefits to helping others. Helping others can often give the client or sponsee a break from obsessing about them self. I see many people in recovery from addiction who use this as a tool to move away from that self-obsession. Helping others helps them. Caution should be taken to ensure that it does not become all-consuming and the person neglects to work on self because of all the others that he/she is helping.

From head to heart

There is a great deal of understanding in the Twelve-Step world about the inadequacy of just intellectualising the Steps. In the *Sponsor's Twelve-Step Manual*, I write about, and use, the process of Bloom's Taxonomy to teach and learn the Steps. This method of teaching is a good way to move knowledge from head to heart and fits in exactly with Twelve-Step philosophy. Remembering something doesn't mean you know it and can use it, apply it to yourself, and help others with it. It needs to go from head to heart. AA has recognised this for a long time and CBT talks about the disconnection between truly believing in something and just thinking it. This spiritual awakening when the intellectual knowledge becomes internalised is spoken of in AA as the moment when someone's eyes come alive, a person has flipped the switch, opened the umbrella, or as in the eternal words of Rex Harrison (*Pygmalion*) is captured in the wonderful sentence; 'By Jove! I think she's got it'.

There are a few ideas that can be of help getting around the 'head to heart' problem. CBT can recommend the 'act as if' approach mentioned in Chapter Eight under the heading 'fake it to make it'. Taking action is also recommended. Both approaches are aware that a person sitting in isolation thinking themselves well does not work. People have to take action. When people experience a belief through taking action they are more likely to appreciate its effects on their emotions. Wishful thinking is just wishful thinking if it's not actioned.

Helping newcomers. In AA, a person really learns the Steps when they sponsor someone else. There is a real jump from intellectualising to applying. The responsibility of looking after another makes a person concentrate hard on getting it right. It is also very reinforcing to watch someone come through the doors of AA, engage in all there is to offer, and then get well. When a new sponsor sees this happen, they internalise the Step at depth and the intuition that is growing in recovery gets stronger. As a side note, I have seen professionals who think AA is a crackpot organisation also change at great depth when for the first time they see the programme in action and experience change and growth in someone, a client, on who they had given up all hope on. This regularly happens and has been documented often.

Goals

CBT is a goal-directed approach to solving issues and problems. In goal setting, CBT recommends identifying what it is a client wants and ask a few questions. Is it because they truly want it or have they been told to do it by another? How is the goal connected to low self-esteem? Have they been conditioned into wanting it? In order for recovery to be truly free, any decisions and choices at this stage in a person's journey have to be honestly owned by them and not be enforced by others. This was not always the case in early recovery.

Now a person has completed the Steps, how far do they want to take their recovery?

There is a good deal of evidence that helping others helps the addict. One person helping another is one of the core principles of AA and so Step Twelve is vital in the process of staying well. Part of the way forward now will be to set goals – a frightening thing for AA people who have been living and learning how to live a day at a time. The reality is that 'not setting goals' is an impossible way of thinking and it's unsustainable for the rest of a person's life. This doesn't mean that certain aspect of a person's recovery can't remain in the 'day at a time' bubble. I know plenty of alcoholics who enjoy long-term recovery and choose the thinking that they only have to 'not drink for today'. Not doing it for the rest of their lives is too much to contemplate. There is a lot to learn about setting goals. There are many pitfalls and the possibility of setting goals too high, or indeed, too low. With all the tools that a person is now able to use in their recovery, the chances of relapse are greatly reduced if not removed altogether.

Living recovery

It is worth mentioning that practising the principles of recovery in all one's 'affairs' is the art of staying well. Attending treatment, doing the Steps in treatment, and then expecting to stay well without any further work is a common misconception that will lead to poor outcomes. Maintenance of this new state of thinking is vital in order to sustain a prolonged new way of life and living. Until thoughts and behaviors become intuitive, as mentioned in the Conscious Competence Model under Step Seven in this book, then a person has to consciously direct their focus and put effort into staying well. As in CBT, which suggests any CBT skills that have been learned require regular practice, the Twelve Steps recognise the same. One of the differences I consider here is that CBT therapy will stop. After your treatment, it is up to you to identify early warning signs, mood changes, or negative thoughts and put in place the techniques and learned skills to halt the progress of this potential downward spiral into relapse. What I have become aware of is that people are not that good at doing that on their own and the Twelve-Step fellowships absolutely recognise this. It's not a case of the Twelve Steps brainwashing people into remaining as members for the rest of their lives. People are welcome to come and go as they please but it is this self-recognition that unless people maintain their attendance at meetings, then there is a potential to be unable to see when these early warning signs creep in. It is shared at meetings many times that when a person stopped attending then eventually they relapsed. AA categorically does not expect obedient long-term attendance at meetings. People have learned and come to see this as a choice is for themselves.

Neuroplasticity

Here is a topic worth mentioning under Step Twelve. Read some of the definitions of this relatively new concept and we learn that you can teach an old dog new tricks. (I hope this short saying translates well in other countries). In fact, there is some vital research around neuroplasticity that is worth noting a little about. Firstly, neuroplasticity is about the brain's ability to reorganise itself and form new neural pathways and, therefore, new thinking. This means that the brain has the capacity to compensate for injury or disease and change the way nerve cells respond. This then means that the diseased thinking, the destructive negatives that have been learned during addiction, the triggers that people react to and the 'old behavior' embedded in one's everyday living, can be changed. But here's the important bit, which is the second part of the equation. Every time we have a thought, do an action or feel a feeling we are reinforcing the neural pathways that have been established. People need new ones and here's the hard bit. It's a bit like going to the gym and building new muscles – no pain, no gain – new thinking will be hard at first. A person's thoughts will be hijacked by old thoughts that have stronger neural pathways. The new way of thinking will be like the Conscious Competence Model covered in Step Seven: 'I know what I'm meant to be doing, but it's really hard'. Keep doing it. Like going to the gym, the repetition will make you stronger. The new ways of thinking will become embedded and natural. A person will reach the levels of intuitive thinking mentioned in the 'Big Book'. They will become easy and natural. A person will no longer have to walk around thinking about 'not thinking' about their drug of choice. For many in early recovery a lot of time and headspace is taken up by trying not to think about drugs or alcohol. The old thinking reduces in power as the neural pathways get weaker and the connections are used less. But they are always there and they never disappear entirely. Drink or drug again and in many people's experience they will fire up like a freshly lit firework and explode into life. Old thinking will return and be at the forefront of one's brain all over again. This is one of the reasons why many people choose to go to meetings for the rest of their lives. They are aware that if they don't constantly reinforce their new way of thinking, by doing all the things Twelve-Step recovery suggests, then it isn't long before serenity starts to slip away, resentments creep back, and the thought of having a drink becomes more powerful.

Step Twelve conclusion

Giving to others, in a non-materialistic way, is a sure way to build self-esteem, create a sense of identity that involves personal meaning and is the key to long-term change and, therefore, recovery.

A spiritual awakening has many meanings for different people but it mostly means 'a deeply personal, unique process of changing one's attitudes, values, feelings, goals, skills and/or roles... a way of living a satisfying, hopeful and contributing life even with the limitations caused by illness' (Leamy et al, 2011). Whether that means you believe in God now is entirely up to you.

Chapter Thirteen

CBT and Twelve-Step techniques

Further similarities and concepts

In CBT, several different techniques are used to help people examine thoughts and behaviors. In the Twelve Steps, these techniques are used repeatedly but no reference is given to therapy, they are just part of the process. Below is a list with some explanations.

Cognitive rehearsal

In CBT, the client imagines a difficult situation and the therapist guides him through the step-by-step process of facing and successfully dealing with it. The client works on practising, or rehearsing, these difficult situations mentally or in role play. So, when the situation arises in real life, the client will draw on the rehearsed behavior to address it.

In Twelve Steps, the sponsee will discuss difficult situations and the sponsor will talk through solutions or actions to take. So, when the situation arises in real life, the sponsee will draw on the rehearsed behavior to address it.

Both approaches, if asked, will help a person through real-life situations by escorting them through that situation. Twelve-Step sponsors do this for free and would even go with a person to help them through a challenging situation such as a wedding reception.

Journaling

In CBT, clients can be asked to keep a detailed journal recounting their thoughts, feelings, and actions when specific situations arise. The journal helps to make the client aware of his or her maladaptive thoughts and shows them the consequences of their behavior. In later stages of therapy, it may serve to demonstrate and reinforce positive behaviors.

In Twelve Steps, people are asked to keep a diary. Steps Ten and Eleven ask people to take a personal inventory and reflect on their day, good or bad. The diary helps to make the sponsee aware of his or her maladaptive thoughts and shows them the consequences of their behavior. In particular, Steps Ten and Eleven ask people to continue to take a personal inventory and reflect on their behavior, both good and bad.

Modelling

In CBT, the therapist and client engage in role-playing exercises in which the therapist acts out appropriate behaviors or responses to situations.

In Twelve Steps, modelling starts in Twelve-Step meetings and continues on a one-to-one basis. There are numerous modelling situations within Twelve-Step meetings. Sponsors lead by example showing the sponsee what to do in regards to meeting format, one person speaking at a time, no cross sharing, not rising to aggression, and many more differing situations.

Conditioning

In CBT, the therapist uses reinforcement to encourage a particular behavior. For example, a person gets a gold star (or an appropriate reward) every time he stays focused on tasks and accomplishes certain daily chores. The gold star reinforces and increases the desired behavior by identifying it with something positive.

In Twelve Steps the sponsor uses reinforcement to encourage a particular behavior. In Twelve-Step meetings, people are greeted warmly, congratulated on achieving certain milestones, and feel valued for the effort they put in. They get positive rewards for the successes that occur.

Reinforcement can also be used to discourage unwanted behaviors by imposing negative consequences.

Systematic desensitisation

In CBT, clients imagine, or experience, a situation they fear, while the therapist employs techniques to help the client relax, helping the person cope with their fear reaction and eventually eliminating the anxiety altogether.

In Twelve-Step meetings, people talk about alcohol/drugs. After being exposed to this for a while the anxiety associated with this eventually dissipates. Talking of alcohol or drugs at a meeting will initially raise anxiety but because nothing untoward happens this eventually leads to the elimination of those thoughts. What does that mean? You get used to it. Why is that important? Because addicts have a mental obsession with their drug of choice. People in early recovery from alcohol often talk about how fearful it is to go to the supermarket and see the mountains of alcohol. This is often talked about in meetings and strategies are discussed on how to deal with this.

There are similarities here to Stress Inoculation Therapy (SIT) in that SIT helps people to prepare for stressful events, educates them on how to cope with stress and learn to control their reactions when confronted by the situation.

Validity testing

In CBT, clients are asked to test the validity of the automatic thoughts they encounter. The therapist may ask the client to defend or produce evidence that a thought is true. If the client is unable to meet the challenge, the faulty nature of the thoughts is exposed.

In Twelve Steps, people are challenged on their automatic thoughts and find they are not valid. Twelve-Step meetings often cover such topics as: 'I can't live without drugs or booze' or 'I will never be happy again'. And one I have heard mentioned many times, 'I can't open the mail without being well and truly drunk.'

Chapter Fourteen
Thought forms

What are the similarities?

Identifying the different sections

Thought forms, commonly used in CBT, come in many shapes and sizes and there any different types that can be targeted to the needs of the individual. For this exercise, I'm choosing a nine-sectioned thought form that is relevant to the progression I often see in Twelve-Step recovery. I'm going to relate these sections to a story that highlights each area. This story covers a persons journey through a certain situation and reveals how she learned to deal with it by going to fellowships meetings and listening. It can be difficult to understand that something as seemingly insignificant as a text can be a trigger for relapse, especially if that person has an extremely poor history with their relationship with alcohol. Unfortunately the power that addiction has over a person can easily lead that person to pick up a drink again even if **we** consider the reasons for picking up that drink trivial.

Section One – Trigger event

Our person is at the cinema and has underestimated the length of the adverts prior to the film and therefore is taking longer than expected. In the cinema, she gets a text from her husband: Where are you?

So, that's our **trigger**. How do the two different models address this?

In CBT, the client will write the trigger down on the thought form in preparation for a discussion with the therapist.

In Twelve Steps, a sponsee may keep a diary of such things or will take note of them in a Tenth Step inventory. Then, either at a meeting or with a sponsor the trigger events will be discussed.

Section Two – Belief

In our story, our person said that were she not actively engaging in her recovery her belief was that she would expect to get angry and drink as a result of the text, and indeed had done so in the past.

In CBT, the client will write down what their expectations, assumptions, and experiences are when the trigger is perceived. This will then be discussed in a session.

In Twelve Steps, either at a meeting or with a sponsor, people share their experiences of how their beliefs dictated their expectations when events happened.

Section Three – Thoughts

When the text came through, our person's first thoughts were, 'He's checking up on me and thinks I'm drinking. I'll show him.'

At this point, I just want to interject with a few thinking errors that may be at play.

1. **Rationalisation:** 'I've a right to be angry. He doesn't trust me'.

2. **Displacement:** 'I'll show him' is often a thought that an addict has. This often results in them using again and both end up getting hurt.

3. **Catastrophising:** 'He's texting me because he really wants to divorce me.'

4. **Mind reading:** 'I Know what he's thinking about me.'

5. **Feelings are not facts:** She feels anxious and mistakes this for cravings and thinks that she must drink again to cope with the situation.

In CBT, the client will write down the thoughts that occurred as the result of the trigger and beliefs, ready to discuss them with the counsellor.

In Twelve Steps, either at a meeting or with a sponsor, people will discuss the resultant thoughts.

Section Four – Consequences.

Our person says that she had many of the thoughts highlighted above but did not respond in the habitual way she normally did (get drunk). In this case, she didn't pick up a drink and text to say she's running late she'll be home shortly.

In CBT, the client will write down what happened as a result of the situation. They will also often rate, on a scale of one to ten, the consequences and the outcomes. This may include things like the behaviors, reactions, and interactions that happened as a result of the situation. These ratings will become the centre of the next session's therapy.

In Twelve Steps, either at a meeting or with a sponsor, people will openly talk about the consequences of their actions including all the various reactions and interactions. The way in which people are able to change those consequences and talk about them openly is usually progressive.

Section Five – Feelings

In a meeting, our person discussed how she felt while all of this was going on. 'I wanted to pick up a drink,' she said, 'but I didn't let those feelings get the better of me.'

In CBT, the client will write down, usually on a scale of one to ten, how this made them feel in regards to various aspects of their feelings. For example, on a scale of one to ten where one is totally calm and ten is full of panic.

In Twelve Steps, either at a meeting or with a sponsor, people will discuss how they felt when all of this was going on and what tools they applied so as to not pick up a drink.

Section Six - Question

In CBT, the therapist will play devil's advocate by asking questions so as to analyse the 'thoughts and consequences' sections. In effect, providing contrary arguments for the thoughts in these sections.

In Twelve Steps, questioning a person across a meeting is not acceptable. A sponsor may raise questions at a later time, however, as people learning the programme listen, they start to hear people talking about the contrary arguments for their own thinking that the person listening could apply to them self. They hear people admitting they were wrong in their behaviors and actions and start to question their own. Often, people in long-term Twelve-Step recovery can be very direct in providing contrary arguments to newcomers.

Section Seven – New answer

Our person came to a new answer saying that, 'It was me and my reactions that made the mountain out of the molehill.'

In CBT, the client will write down any new answers as a result of the previous work discussed and celebrate it with their therapist.

In Twelve Steps, either at a meeting or with a sponsor, people will share the answer they found to their problem thinking. This will be reinforced by the positive reactions they get from others at the meeting.

Section Eight – New consequences

So, what were those consequences for our person? When she got home she was a little nervous but found out that her husband had been concerned because of an announcement on the local radio station. It had been reported that there had been a serious accident on a route she could have taken and her husband was getting worried. She had taken longer at the cinema and was unaware of the accident and did not know this was the cause of her husbands concern.

In CBT, the client will write down any new consequences that have resulted or will result, from doing this work.

In Twelve Steps, in group or at meetings, people will share about the consequences of their new thinking. Again, this will be celebrated and reinforced by others at the meeting. At the opposite end to this, if a strategy failed, then persons in the meeting will offer support and share their experiences of coping with a similar scenario.

Section Nine – New feelings

In the meeting, she discussed the feelings of freedom and relief that she now felt. She could clearly differentiate from the usual feelings that would result if she had only listened to her first thoughts about her husband and picked up a drink.

In CBT, the client will, often on a scale of one to ten, rate how they believe this new strategy has made them feel.

In Twelve Steps, in group or at meetings, people will talk about how they feel now and this is usually reinforced with friendly and warm praise.

In conclusion, we see that this simple thought form, used by many professionals, mirrors the processes that happen naturally in Twelve-Step recovery. No direct therapeutic intervention is happening and no one is directed to follow this process. It has occurred naturally as part of one's progression.

A thinking error minefield

I received a telephone call from a person at about 3 am and, of course, answered it as any member of a mutual aid fellowship would. (For all you budget holders, yes, we do this for free.) The person involved has given permission to highlight all the thinking errors as they were related to me.

At 3am, I received a call from a person concerned that someone on a bus had broken her anonymity in front of work colleagues. There had been a work's award ceremony, which she attended and, on the way home, a passenger, who was drunk, blurted out 'Haven't I seen you at meetings?' By 3am, this person was in sheer panic and had **catastrophised** the event into the end of the world.

(I'm not belittling that response, it was incredibly powerful for the person going through it.) We talked for a short while then re-engaged at about 7am. By that time and with a bit of help from the thinking error of **fortune telling,** she was utterly convinced that all her colleagues would know that she went to 'meetings' by the return of work Monday morning. We talked at length and the anxiety subsided. Later she phoned to tell me she had written her resignation as she knew she would now get laid off once the general manager found out. 'I know what he thinks like,' was mentioned. A common thinking error called **mind reading** was now at play. After talking for some time, I persuaded her not to hand in the resignation and just see what happens. There is no point in jumping before you are pushed.

By the Monday evening when she phoned, she had ventured into the **personalising** error. She now believed she should be dismissed as all the problems and difficulties at her place of work were probably all caused by her or could be traced back to her. 'I might as well leave now,' she told me. I reminded her that **feelings were not facts** and that because she was in a heightened state of anxiety, self-blame was easy at the moment. She calmed down and continued going to work, suspicions started to creep in that her work colleagues were all waiting for a big announcement of her dismissal but doubt about this was starting to get a foothold; nothing had happened yet. On the Thursday, the error of **disqualifying the positive** had a little flare up with the person phoning me up to say that the general manager had spoken to her really nicely and friendly and had congratulated her on her work. 'He's obviously setting me up for the big fall,' she said. 'He wants to see me tomorrow. I don't know how I'm gonna sleep.' The meeting with the boss went great, she had been called in to be told that they (her place of work) had noticed how much her work had improved over the last six months (since she had stopped drinking) and as a result, she would not be on the list of compulsory redundancies being announced.

Then the weekend hit and we had a similar but smaller roller coaster ride of thinking errors, but it was fine. No one ever mentioned the drunk on the bus and now three years later she looks back and smiles at this bumpy episode. Her recovery is in top form and her responsibilities at work have expanded leading her to work in new and exciting areas. "People don't know I've got a problem" she says.

People don't know I've got a problem

I hear many tales and stories along the same lines: 'I can't go to a meeting in case someone finds out'. Well, I've got news for you, they most probably already know. Recently, I heard of a person in an addiction hostel on a detox saying that she couldn't go to meetings in case her neighbours found out she had a drinking problem. A close and trusted friend had to remind her that nearly all of her neighbours already knew. She had given the game away herself with various behaviors: falling asleep on the front lawn, throwing up in the flower border, forgetting to turn the music off and staggering down the middle of the road were to name but a few.

So why do people think others don't know? What is the fear of bumping into someone you may know at a meeting all about? What's going on in the addict's mind? Is their denial so strong that they believe no one anywhere knows? Probably. From hiding bottles when living alone to drinking in front of another but telling them you're not, there is plenty of strange addictive behavior that goes on. There is plenty of strange psychology that goes with addiction and denial is a twisty and complex enemy.

People talk about -isms – no, that's not a typo. So, what is an -ism? These are odd behaviors people associate with their addiction. Quirks of behavior, character defects, shortcomings, predictable behaviors, manipulation, downright lying are all things that addicts in recovery will recognise. The list goes on but one thing is for sure, they are very, very common to many people with a substance problem.

Maybe the fear of being found out is connected to the reality of having to accept the problem oneself. A person can maintain their denial if no one confronts them with the problem. Going to meetings means that the acknowledgement of an addiction has been formalised and can no longer be declared untrue. It's very sad that this denial, this refusal to engage, this inability to realise that status won't help a fatal illness. The fear of being seen will most probably wreck that person's life and in the end, everyone will know anyway, probably including the local police department, etc.

'I can't talk in groups,' is another reason given not to attend. When scrutinized, the groups people can't talk in are selective. They can talk in front of family, groups of friends, to work colleagues, or in business meetings. What is difficult is the potential of talking in front of others about vulnerabilities, exposing one's inner self to others, about admitting something that they are highly embarrassed about or feel shame around.

There are no expectations in Twelve-Step meetings to say anything if you don't wish to. Even in groups that like to do a round-the-room introduction of themselves, it is perfectly OK to say 'pass'.

In time, people will choose to engage but it is worth remembering that the pressure people say they feel they are under to speak at meetings is usually self-imposed. A friend in long-term recovery, a guy with over twenty-five years, tells me that it took him two years of attending meetings before he spoke his first word.

Final conclusions

It doesn't matter whether you're a believer or not. If you believe in other models of recovery and dismiss the Twelve Step one. Whether you have a faith in a religious God or no faith at all. The simple truth is that AA and the Twelve-Step approach has worked for millions of people. And, yes, there is plenty of evidence for that.

Addiction is such a killer disease that it should be declared an epidemic of significant proportions. If it were any other disease, the whole world would be in a panic and rushing to find a cure.

The processes that are described in this book are how I see them and I'm sure I will come under fire from some and be praised by others but this is the nature of it. Like addiction and recovery, there are multiple layers within the illness, different drivers, incredible variables in social status, physical differences, cultural differences and the list goes on and on. The point is some will like the approaches I have described and some will not.

To finish:

'There is a principle which is a bar against all information, which is proof against all arguments, and which cannot fail to keep a man in everlasting ignorance—that principle is contempt prior to investigation.' (various authors).

Bibliography

Williams, C.J. (2001) Overcoming Depression. London: Arnold. —— & Garland, A. (2002) Identifying and challenging unhelpful thinking: a Five Areas approach. Advances in Psychiatric Treatment, 8, in press.

The Magic of Thinking Big by David Schwartz. Read more at http://www.pickthebrain.com/blog/grow-the-action-habit/#RJ8v8HFVCcUVlaQe.99

Rogers, Carl R. (1957). The Necessary and Sufficient Conditions of Therapeutic Personality Change. Journal of Consulting Psychology, 21. Retrieved from http://www.shoreline.edu/dchris/psych236/Documents/Rogers.pdf

Amanda McCorquodale Feb 2016 *Fake it to make it.* Accessed 18 Jun 2018. - http://mentalfloss.com/article/74310/8-fake-it-til-you-make-it-strategies-backed-science.

Serenity prayer - http://www.amybucherphd.com/psychology-and-the-serenity-prayer/

Talking - https://www.forbes.com/sites/alicegwalton/2014/06/03/11-intriguing-reasons-to-give-talk-therapy-a-try/#7ca3f65b4ebb

Bartholomew, N. G., & Simpson, D. D. (2005). Unlock your thinking, open your mind. Fort Worth: Texas Christian University, Institute of Behavioral Research. Available: the IBR Website: www.ibr.tcu.edu

https://www.thecabinchiangmai.com/understanding-and-working-aa-s-12-steps-using-cognitive-behavioral-therapy/

New York University. "Is there such a thing as an emotional hangover? Researchers find that there is." ScienceDaily. ScienceDaily, 26 December 2016. www.sciencedaily.com/releases/2016/12/161226211238.htm

Conceptual framework for personal recovery in mental health: systematic review and narrative synthesis. Leamy M, Bird V, Le Boutillier C, Williams J, Slade M. King's College London, Health Service and Population Research Department, Institute of Psychiatry.

http://www.brainworksneurotherapy.com/what-neuroplasticity

Alcoholics Anonymous, 3rd edition. New York: Alcoholics Anonymous World Services Inc, 1976. (The "Big Book.")

Twelve Steps and Twelve Traditions, New York. Alcoholics Anonymous World Services Inc, 1981. (The "Twelve and Twelve")

Further works by J Elford

The Sponsor's 12 Step Manual

The Sponsor's 12 Step Manual is an independent approach to delivering the program of A.A. that will help people learn faster and remember more.

The manual uses a six-point method of teaching (Bloom's Taxonomy)to reinforce learning and to increase comprehension and promote awareness of the Steps to its fullest extent.

The process starts with remembering and understanding the language used in the Steps then progresses on to an in depth study of what is in A.A. literature. The six levels also cover self reflection and creativity with the final level of each Step looking at how a sponsee may carry the message to a newcomer.

These are not 'stand alone' books, for them to work you will also need to have access to A.A.s Big Book and The 12 Steps and 12 Traditions.

There is a Workbook Edition of The Sponsor's 12 Step Manual in which additional space has been added for writing answers.

The Sponsor's 12 Traditions Manual is an approach to understanding the traditions of A.A. using the same methodology of Bloom's taxonomy as above and again this will help people learn faster and remember more. This leads to greater understanding of the information in the 12 Traditions. This is not a stand alone book, you will need to have access to he 12 Steps and 12 Traditions in order to use this book.

These books have achieved worldwide sales.

The Integrated Step Course

The Integrated Step Course is a 3 - 6 month programme designed for drug and alcohol treatment facilities. It is based around the 12 Steps.   ·

The Integrated Step Course is a unique and powerful tool for use in treatment centres and rehabs. It's a practical, interactive, step-by-step system that guides both staff and client through a recordable and evidence based programme! It gets people focused on what there is to learn and sets standards that everyone can be satisfied with, bringing strategy alive and making learning truly engaging! This is a MUST if you are running a treatment centre anywhere in the world....

There are two manuals covering all twelve steps. This includes, in total, 72 lesson plans - 6 per Step, over 180 pages of questions in the Client Questions section, 24 Power point presentations, 32 Activity Maps and 72 Group Facilitator Prompters. In total there are 180 individual sessions that can take up to 316 hours of face to face learning.

WISC R.I.

Our newly designed WISC R.I. programme has been developed for those centres that are smaller with less or part time staff. It was developed at the request of one of the major UK prisons who wanted to run the course alongside other major programs they were running.

It is a reduced intensity version of our Integrated Step Course.

WISC R.I is designed to deliver three sessions a week at two hours a session over 12 weeks and includes client homework to be completed in personal time.

For more information on any of these works got to www.getinotrecovery.com

Made in the USA
Columbia, SC
10 July 2018